Acclaim for Sean Dietrich

"Dietrich is a Southern Garrison Keillor." — *Southern Living*

'Sean Dietrich is Southern storytelling at its finest; reading his words is like sitting on a front porch with a Mason jar of sweet tea, listening to your uncle weave a story you know in your heart is true, but there's a little magic thrown in too." — Annie B. Jones, author of *Ordinary Time*

"Southern Literature at its finest." — *Southern Literary Review*

"His style is easy, inviting us to laugh out loud on occasion. Others touch our hearts deeply. His expressive use of vocabulary reminds me of Norman Rockwell, painting instead with a pen."— *Galveston Daily News*

"Dietrich's sense of humor and openness to others adds layers of richness to the text... [he] cleverly illustrates the importance of maintaining relationships, keeping promises, and being true to oneself."

— *Kirkus Reviews*

"Nobody writes quite like Sean Dietrich. He is the master of storytelling, no question, and he writes with rich, lyrical phrases... and deep insight into the human psyche." — *Southern Literary Review*

"Sean Dietrich's sentences are the crack cocaine of literary humor... if you liked Lewis Grizzard, you will love Sean Dietrich!"
— Andy Andrews, *New York Times* bestselling author of *The Traveler's Gift*

"A master storyteller, able to create viscerally real characters that leap from the page." — *Reader's Digest*

"Sean Dietrich can spin a story." — *Southern Living*

"A spark of hope to those who need it." — *Library Journal*

"Mesmerizing... with a riches of complex characters and lyrical language."
— *Kirkus Reviews* (Starred Review for *Stars of Alabama*)

"Dietrich has a lovely, seasoned voice that's anchored by his deep understanding of the charm and depth of the South."
— Boo Walker, bestselling author of *A Spanish Sunrise*

"Make no mistake. ... [Dietrich is] an expert storyteller."
— Shawn Smucker, author of *Light from Distant Stars*

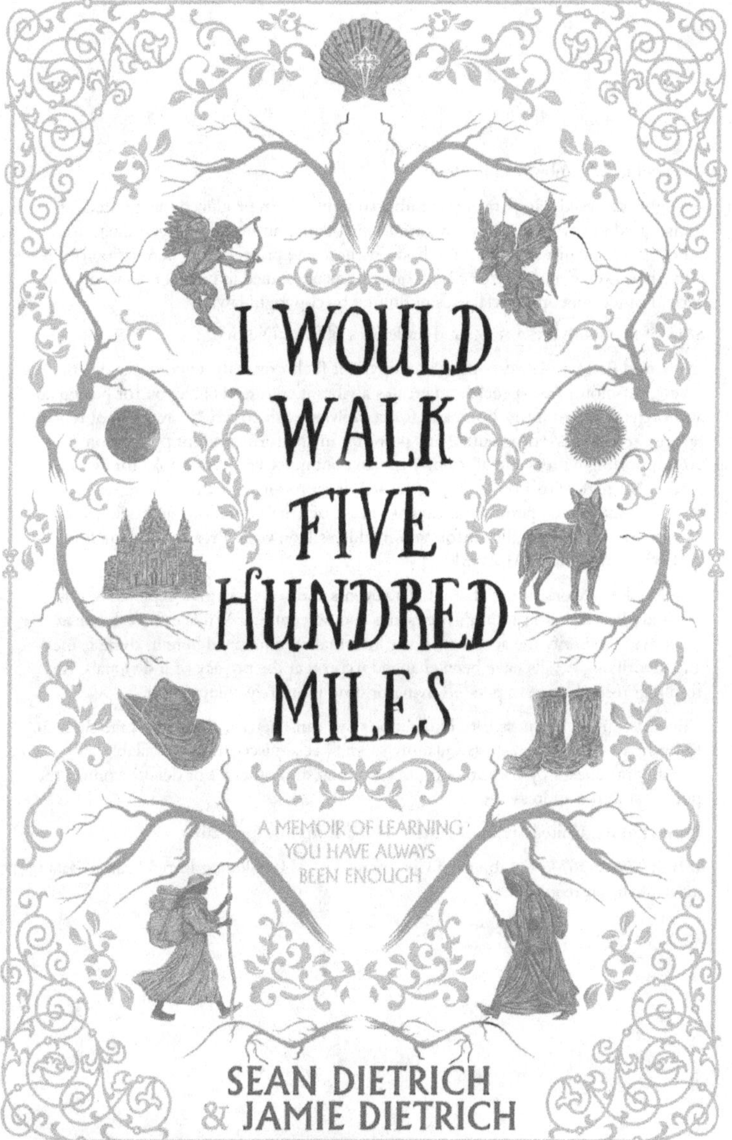

I WOULD WALK FIVE HUNDRED MILES

SEAN DIETRICH
& JAMIE DIETRICH

IRONWOOD PRESS

BIRMINGHAM

Cover design by Youness Elh. Illustrations by Sean Dietrich Edited by Julie Breihan. Published by Ironwood Press Quantity sales: Special discounts are available on quantity purchases by corporations, associations, and others. For details, contact the publisher at the address above.

Printed in the United States of America First Edition: April, 2026

ISBN: 9798253677247 Library of Congress Control Cataloging-in-publication data is available upon request.

FOREWORD

On a soaking-wet Monday in May 2025, my friend Akkie and I stood at a bus stop in Spain—or something that passed for one. We skipped two Camino stages by bus to take a rest day, because the day before I had run straight into a wall.

After we had waited a while, a man in sandals walked up. Red hair, a red beard and mustache, and a violin case in his hand. In some ways he looked like a pilgrim, but sandals on a rainy day, and a violin case, felt unusual.

My friend asked him about both. He told us about his Camino, his leg injury, but mostly about his fiddle, American folk music, theater performances, and writing. In fifteen minutes a warm bond formed between us.

What struck me deeply was that he was a professional author. Not long before, my first collection of prayer poems had been accepted by a publisher, yet I still did not dare dream of a writing career. One reason for my Camino was to gather courage to find a new path after burnout.

When I told him about my love for writing and my book, he asked me to read a prayer from my manuscript in my own language, Dutch. There in the Spanish downpour I heard myself read one of my poems aloud for the first time in my life, and suddenly the fire inside me lit.

The bus arrived. While Akkie talked with Sean and an Irish fellow traveler, I looked up Sean's Facebook page and began reading his blogs. As I read, the fire burned brighter: he had climbed from a valley, followed his passions—why shouldn't I try?

Now, almost a year later, I am turning writing into my profession. That is what walking the Camino can do. You share life's deepest questions with strangers, and somehow, in the rhythm of walking through nature and in those chance encounters with people of all kinds of cultures and philosophies, answers may appear. Some people cross your path again and again; others you meet once and never again. But walking the Camino can give you new insights, fresh courage, and open new directions.

I hope and pray that as a reader of this beautiful book by Sean, you too may experience a pilgrim's journey of your own.

Buen Camino.

—Lidy Torenbeek, 2025

I WOULD WALK

FIVE HUNDRED MILES

PRÓLOGO

EFORE I TELL YOU OF CAMINOS, CASTLES, AND cathedrals, of beautiful maidens, wicked giants, brave pilgrims, and knights of old; before I speak of angels and devils, teachers and disciples, lords and ladies, butchers, bakers, and candlestick makers, or long walks through the mists and mountains of ancient Spain, I want to tell you about a little boy with severely buck teeth and carrot-red hair.

He is a chubby boy. With lots of freckles. And a deep, abiding love for Little Debbie products. He is a first baseman. A fisherman. A lightly decorated Boy Scout. And is widely known throughout the region for possessing the uniquely awe-inspiring ability of riding his bike with no hands.

Right now, the little boy is looking out his window. As the last funeral visitor leaves the old family farmhouse. A rooster tail of dust rises behind the back tires of a departing F-100 pickup. Dust drifts upward into the heavens like ether. The vehicle disappears over the horizon. The visitation service is officially over.

The boy is wearing all black. Black tie. Black trousers. His hair is slicked to his head with Aunt Verna's own spit. His Kmart shoes are cutting off circulation to his feet.

Currently, his aunt is opening all the windows to let his

daddy's spirit escape. This is just what we do, his aunt says. Nobody knows why. Or if they know, they forgot to tell his aunt because she won't answer when he asks. His aunt is talking to herself as she works. She makes happy small, humming noises around the house, as if nothing is wrong.

The boy leaves his perch at the window and peels out of his black polyester. Then he walks into his closet, half naked, shuts the door behind him, and sits on the floor. He knows this is an odd thing to do, sitting mostly naked in the closet. But he just feels so lost.

Spears of light peek through the slatted closet doors, and he sits and cries. He wishes he was dead. This is the first time he has ever wished for death. He feels guilty because he knows there is probably something in the Bible about how wishing you were dead is a sin.

He rests his head on something hard and rigid. It is an old fiddle case. The fiddle used to be his grandfather's. His grandfather is dead. So is his grandmother. A few of his uncles are gone. And now his father too.

Everyone is dead.

The boy hears a *thump, thump, thump* in the hall. His baby sister will not stop pacing. He doesn't know why she won't sit down and cry like the rest of them. But she won't. She keeps looking for Daddy. Where is Daddy? she keeps asking. Where did he go? The boy repeatedly tells his sister that Daddy is dead, get it through your thick skull, dammit. Then he has to hold his sister and apologize for saying *dammit*. She cries into his chest.

This is all just part of the grieving, his aunt says. Totally normal. People have to grieve, she says.

The boy doesn't know how his aunt knows so much about death. Maybe his aunt really does know everything, like she often claims.

Last week the boy's father tried to kill them all. It is an event the boy's brain keeps replaying. He's been having this dream every time he sleeps since. The dream keeps repeating. Every night. Same dream. Each nap. Same dream. It's all he sees. It is all he will see until his late thirties.

In the dream, his crazed father wanders upstairs holding a pistol. Daddy has just gotten off work, still covered in soot from welding iron column splices all day. The boy's father holds the revolver to his mother's temple.

Strangely, the gun is covered with the boy's striped T-shirt. Why? the boy wonders. What's the point of covering the gun? His father got the shirt out of the laundry hamper because that's where the boy left it. Because the boy's mother always made them put dirty clothes in the hamper. Because his mother was not everyone's laundry fairy, for heaven's sake. Because God did not put mothers on earth to cook and clean and wipe everyone's butts, for the love of all that is good and holy, so pick up your clothes once in a while. Where were you raised, a barn? Jesus, Mary, and the donkey too, put your clothes in the hamper.

When the boy sees his father point that gun at his mother, the boy's insides turn to water. Then his father leads his mom out to the porch, like an animal. Shoving, pushing, beating, and pistol-whipping. Mama goes willingly. She has already been beaten until her teeth are loosened. Plus, Daddy says if she doesn't follow him to the porch, he'll kill her children next.

Who was that man? That wasn't Daddy. That wasn't the coach of the boy's Little League team. That wasn't his troop leader. That wasn't the same guy who sang in church choir.

What happened to this man's brain?

The boy can hear his mother's body banging around on the floorboards. The boy's sister is crying. Something has to be done. The boy has no choice but to rush into the garage, unzip his father's hunting rifle, and remove it from the case. The boy stands on an overturned bucket. He trains the sight on his father, aiming through a glass window in the garage.

The boy's parents are now outside. Daddy is holding the pistol against the base of his mother's head. The boy trains the sight on his father. He is about to end this man's life. Amazingly, the boy isn't crying. Too much adrenaline. Although he is shaking so much he can hardly keep his finger on the trigger. He knows, too, that he *must* pull this trigger. He must. Or his mom is a goner. His little eleven-year-old brain accepts this, and this moment changes his brain forever. He will be broken after this.

He pulls the trigger.

But nothing happens.

No gunshot.

Maybe the safety is still on.

Maybe it is a misfire.

The boy will never know. Either way, something intervened during this moment of horror. This moment that is both the worst moment of the child's life, but also the greatest and most sacred. Somehow. It is a moment unlike any other the boy has known. Or will ever know.

For the air has become electrified; the boy's hair is standing up. Like static electricity has just filled the room. It is a heavenly feeling. A secure feeling. The feeling of complete, existential love. Like a huge blanket is being wrapped around him. Like a mother hen, guarding its chicks.

Miraculously, his mother escapes the mad gunman. She runs through the woods. She lives.

The deputies arrest the boy's father. While they place his dad into the back seat of the cruiser, other deputies search in the garage. They find the rifle the boy was holding. The boy is scared to death. The boy just knows that he is about to go to prison for life. No, of course not, the deputies say. Nobody's going to jail, son. Any brave little boy would've done the exact same for their mama. But the boy feels black all over. Tainted. Full of shame.

He hopes they don't tell his father about the gun. He doesn't want his dad to dislike him. He hopes they don't tell his mom. This would break her heart.

Daddy goes to jail. His father sits there for a long time, in a cell, until the boy's uncle bails him out. The next morning the boy's father's body is found in his brother's garage. Self-inflicted gunshot wound. His big toe was stuck in the trigger guard of a shotgun.

The boy looks around the dark closet.

He has that warm-blanket feeling again. It's happening right here. Right now. Like something is hugging him. So the boy just goes with it. The boy hugs himself and weeps, rocking himself. He has no idea where this warm feeling is coming from, or why it's happening. The feeling is love. Love so thick, so smothering, so encompassing, it almost suffocates him. Love so deep he almost can't tell which direction is up or down. Love so powerful, he can hardly feel his body anymore. Love so sweet, it must be diluted or it would be too strong to bear.

Then a voice speaks. It is a real voice. An actual sound the boy hears with his physical ears. A voice that is small and still. The voice of whoever is holding him. So faint, he almost misses it. But strong, nonetheless. It is a woman's voice. Rich and eternally maternal. Like a mother.

"I've got you," the voice says.

The boy just rocks himself to sleep.

I've got you.

And this is where our tale begins.

April 8, 2025

We leave for Spain tomorrow—
to walk 500 miles. I bought this
leather-bound journal after my
mother died. I needed a place
to put my thoughts. I'm not
the most consistent writer, but I
try.

Embossed on the front of the
journal is a quote from A.A.
Milne. The quote says:

"If ever there is a tomorrow
when we're not together,
there is something you must

always remember. You are braver than you believe, stronger than you seem and smarter than you think. But the most important thing is, even if we're apart, I'll always be with you."

As we embark on this pilgrimage tomorrow, I am looking ahead with open eyes and heart.

—Jamie Dietrich

Libro Uno

I T'S JUST A ROAD. THAT'S ALL IT WILL EVER BE. That's all it *can* be. A really, *really* long road. Nothing more. I think.

I mean, how can a simple dirt path be anything more? How can a highway of gravel and mud and pavement be other-worldly? It can't be. It's impossible. Just forget it.

So whatever else is said about the Camino de Santiago within this book, whatever fantastical claims are made by others, myself included, whatever lore and fables are oft associated with this road through Spain, whatever stories shall be told throughout the ages to come, whatever abstruseness surrounds the Camino, we must first truthfully and seriously ask ourselves, "What the heck does *abstruseness* mean?"

Then we must remind ourselves that it's just a road.

This is important to remember because a lot of things happen on this road. People's lives are changed. Clarity is found. Miracles are seen. Magic is felt. And yet pilgrims errantly attribute such mysteries to the road itself, forgetting that a byway like the Camino is merely soil and dust. Earth and grit. Mineral and dirt. Still, many pilgrims fall onto their hands and knees and kiss the ground during profound moments on this trail. I have seen them do this. I have done this.

But in the end, as I say, it's just a road.

Granted, it is one of earth's most famous roads. One of the three most historic pilgrimage routes known to Western civilization, outdated only by pilgrimage routes to Jerusalem, Rome, and Graceland. This is one of the most fairy-taled thoroughfares in history. There are even rumors that Frank L.

Baum's *Wizard of Oz* borrowed the idea of a yellow brick road from the Camino de Santiago and that the emerald city was a knock-off of the Cathedral of Santiago de Compostela. These rumors are likely not true, however, since I myself have walked the Camino, and not once did I see any members of the Lollipop Guild.

Still, I can see how someone might compare the fabled yellow brick road with the Camino. Both roads lead somewhere special. Both roads are long, winding, and uncertain. And both roads are walked by characters who lack brains.

Take me, for example.

There are a lot of outrageous claims about the Camino. The Camino has allegedly healed disease, cured cancer, won wars, saved lives, brought down government tyranny, resurrected the dead, and on at least one occasion, brought roasted chickens back to life.

I am not kidding. This happened in the Middle Ages, when a young German pilgrim was arrested and hung unjustly for theft while traveling the Camino. After his hanging, his parents, afflicted with grief, continued their pilgrimage to Santiago. On the return trip home, the parents passed the gallows, only to find their son was still swinging from the rope. And he was still alive.

Their son, who was evidently able to speak despite the noose around his neck, said he was just fine and that Saint James had been supporting his body weight so the rope wouldn't kill him and if it wasn't too much trouble, would they mind terribly getting him off these gallows?

The parents rushed across town to the local magistrate, who was just about to eat supper that evening. The magistrate laughed at the parents' claims. "Your son, alive?" the magistrate said, laughing so hard he nearly choked on his food. "Impossible! I watched him hang! Your son is about as alive as these roasted birds on my plate!"

Whereupon, the roasted chickens are said to have sprouted feathers, leapt off the plate, and started crowing before many witnesses. Ever after, devout believers would call this event the "Miracle of the Roasted Chickens." The boy was cut down and freed. He went vegan after that.

Another story.

In the fourteenth century, a blind man named Bernardo, from Apulia, Italy, wanted to walk the Camino de Santiago. Everyone told him this was foolish. From Italy, the distance was 1,500 miles to Santiago. Bernardo found a little beggar boy who guided him on his 1,500-mile pilgrimage. The two traversed mountains, rivers, countrysides, and impossible obstacles. Bernardo walked the whole route, resting his hand on the top of the child's head for guidance.

When they arrived at Santiago, years later, Bernardo entered the cathedral, weeping. He collapsed in awe. Imagine spending years of your life following a beggar child across Europe. Imagine what you would have felt when you finally arrived at your destination.

Bernardo touched the *Pilar de los Croques*, the central pillar of the Portico of Glory in the cathedral of Compostela. This pillar had already been touched by the hands of so many pilgrims over the centuries that a handprint had been worn into the stone. But as Bernardo's fingers slipped into the smooth grooves of the handprint, he felt a flashing heat course through his body. His sight was restored. He lived the rest of his life with sight. He probably went vegan too.

One more. In 2012, Phil Volker was diagnosed with stage-four colorectal cancer. Doctors said he was dying. He had a matter of months left to live, his doctors said. Phil had always wanted to walk the Camino de Santiago, but medical experts emphatically said no, it was too late to walk any Caminos. His body was too weakened. Too sickly. And anyway, there was no way for him to hike in his condition, not while undergoing chemo treatments. Phil could hardly keep food down or stand upright, let alone walk 798 kilometers from France to Spain.

Phil was undaunted. He painstakingly built his own Camino replica in his backyard, constructing a reproduction of the Camino Francés on a ten-acre plot of land behind his home. He calculated that it would take 909 laps on his "Camino" to simulate the route from Saint-Jean-Pied-de-Port to Santiago. And he got busy.

Phil went outside every day to walk his Camino. He walked throughout chemo treatments. He walked through nausea, weight loss, hair loss, vision loss, and heaven-knows-what-else loss. He walked while enduring his own private hell.

Amazingly, Phil's health somehow stabilized throughout his simulated Camino journeys. Nobody could explain this. Whereupon Phil flew to Spain to walk the actual Camino Francés. All five hundred miles. On his own two feet. He completed his first Camino in September of 2014.

Before Phil Volker died in 2021, he completed a total of five Caminos in his own backyard. Since his death, upward of two hundred pilgrims and cancer patients have visited Phil's backyard and walked his Camino, only to find healing and the unexplained disappearance of chemo side effects.

Those few anecdotes are just some of the thousands of stories—maybe hundreds of millions of stories—about the Camino. There are books full of miracles. Many of them are well-documented and confirmed. Told better than I can tell them.

There really is something paranormal about this place. You feel something out there. You don't know what it is you're feeling, but it's there. Watching you. Sometimes you feel like *It* is walking with you. Whatever *It* is. You could swear you hear *Its* footsteps behind you, although you are alone. You might turn to look behind you, but nobody is there in the forest. Just you. Just the birds.

Lost pilgrims often report seeing dogs materialize out of the woods, leading them when they are lost. Then the dogs fall back into the thicket and disappear as easily as they came. During moments of calamity, many pilgrims have claimed to meet strangers who seemingly appear out of nowhere. These unexpected visitors offer help, offer first-aid, give directions, or provide calm in a time of panic. Then the strangers just kind of—poof!—vanish.

Still, there are many perpetuated misconceptions about the Camino. When you talk about the Camino to non-Camino walkers, you can see their faces turn to wood.

The biggest misunderstanding, perhaps, is that the Camino is strictly a religious thing. Which is wrong. There are hundreds of thousands of Camino hikers who visit the trail each year, and many of them are not even the slightest bit religious. There are day hikers, campers, rock climbers, students, geo-tourists, and cyclists who wear tight-fitting, junk-revealing Lycra suits covered in logos of sponsors who do not pay them to ride their bikes. These cyclists hog the entire trail, often coming very close to careening over innocent pedestrian pilgrims while angrily shouting Spanish swear words as they fly past. Great people.

Even so, a lot of people continue to think the Camino is exclusively a Catholic thing. Newcomers say this all the time. "I thought you had to be Catholic to hike the Camino." Nope. You don't. You don't have to be Jewish to visit Jerusalem, you don't have to be Irish to visit Ireland, and you don't have to be missing teeth to visit Waffle House. The Camino is not the Vatican City. The Camino does not belong to a religious denomination or a sect of people who wear pointy hats and use incense as they hike. The Camino belongs to everyone. It belongs to you. It belongs to me.

While on the Camino, you will hike alongside Buddhist monks, Hindus, Latter-Day Saints, Jews, Muslims, Mennonites, Methodists, Presbyterians, Episcopalians, Baptists, agnostics, atheists, former inmates, and even Saint Louis Cardinals fans. We said prayers alongside Korean Taoists, Irish protestants, Upstate New York hippies, and devout Mormon people who openly admit to wearing special underwear as part of their religion. On our Camino journey, we shared bunkrooms with Israelis and Palestinians. We broke bread with Russians and Ukrainians at the same table. We shared wine with Democrats and Republicans. And everyone was at peace. Blacks and whites. Catholics and protestants. Zionists and Iranians. Everyone was on the same path. We all shared the same goals. And our goals were so simple:

Find food. Find water. Find a place to sleep.

Not much has changed in a few thousand years on the Camino. Centuries before Catholicism was even a glint in Constantine's eye, *Homo sapiens* have been walking this path. Primitive Celtic and Iberian tribes walked this route in hopes of finding a better life, navigating by stars, following the *Bealach na Bó Finne*—the Milky Way. The Romans used this road as a trade highway, calling it the *Via Aquitania*. People from all over the world journeyed the Camino until its original end at Cape Finisterre, "The End of the World." Whereupon pilgrims would stand at the Atlantic, wind on their faces, staring into the edge of forever, pondering the great human questions of existence. Who are we? Why are we here? Are these multiple choice questions?

Chronologically, the Camino has seen everything six thousand years of human civilization has to offer. It has been a perpetual hotbed of disagreement; the center of controversy, religious wars, endless political upheavals, espionage, and genocide; the epicenter of the Roman Conquest of Hispania; an integral part of the Reconquista; a political game piece during the Hundred Years' War and the Spanish Civil War. The Camino has seen the rise and fall of empires, feudalism, monarchism, industrialism, commercialism, and the technological revolution. The route has been outlawed by kings, banned by governments, and written about by scholars, poets, and quasi-literate fools, such as yours truly.

The apostle James is believed to have walked this path two thousand years ago to deliver the gospel to the Galicians. Saint Francis of Assisi walked this path with his bare feet and fell down before Santiago and wept. Dante walked this pathway before writing a bestseller that would exhaustively and thoroughly freak everyone out. Two popes have walked the Camino. US president John Adams walked this road. Thousands of Jewish refugees, fleeing Nazi Germany, desperate to escape the Holocaust, found shelter in the Pyrenees on the Camino. And as if all of this isn't reason enough, Justin Timberlake has walked the Camino.

This verdant history lends a kind of mysticism to the trail. Maybe this is why you sense a "deep knowing" while on the trail. Most pilgrims sense this knowing. Many speak of the Camino as though it knows them, understands them, and communicates with them. As though the trail were alive, with a mind of its own. "The Camino provides" is a common phrase on the Camino. "The Camino will not give you what you want, only what you need" is another maxim. "If the Camino wills it" is a sentence you will hear a lot. And my favorite inspirational phrase: "The Camino will send all inconsiderate trail cyclists to everlasting hell."

Which I'd like to believe is true.

So, it doesn't matter which religion, creed, or persuasion you are. It doesn't matter whether you believe in supernatural things or not. Whether you are reading this book or whether you are walking the physical road, the Camino is yours. For the Camino is not a geographical location at all. It is not a 500-mile section through the splendor of Spain. The Camino is here. The Camino is now. The Camino is *this*, everything you see. All this *thisness* is the Camino of Life, which you are walking currently. Once you give yourself permission to understand the significance of your life's journey—boom!—you are on the Camino.

Which is why many people report suddenly discovering who they really are out on the Camino. People break down on the side of the road, weeping at various shrines. Relationships are put back together. People fall in love. Pilgrims who have contemplated suicide often credit the Camino for calling them back from the edge. Those who never believed in a god realize they already knew the Divine, and have loved this higher power throughout their entire lifetime.

One afternoon we were walking the Camino when there appeared directly before us, smack-dab in the middle of the Camino path, a rushing creek. The creek was wide and deep. There were many jagged rocks. The water was frothed white with foam. We pilgrims would certainly need to help each other when crossing this creek or we would face-plant. The recent rains had made the rushing torrent too high for safe passage.

On the far banks of the creek, there were three Franciscan monks who had just crossed to the other side. They were all wearing daypacks over their woolen robes.

"Excuse me!" I cried out. "Could one of you help me to the other side?"

An older monk stepped to the water's edge and looked at me from across the small river. His face was radiant. "You're already on the other side, brother," said the monk with a playful grin.

He was only joking, of course. But his words smacked of an ancient parable. I felt as though scales had fallen from my eyes. The friar was right. There is nothing left to do. There is nothing left to know. There are no magic prayers to make. No dotting of any proverbial *i*'s, no crossing of any allegorical *t*'s. You have all you need.

You're already on the other side, brother.

And so, in a way, the Camino is still restoring vision to the blind, as it did centuries ago. Dead things are still being raised. Each day a new resurrection is made. Each morning a new life is found. Whatever is out there, it's real. But please remember, despite all I've just told you, as I say, it's still just a road. That's all it is. That's all it can ever be. The Camino is just lifeless, inanimate dirt.

I think.

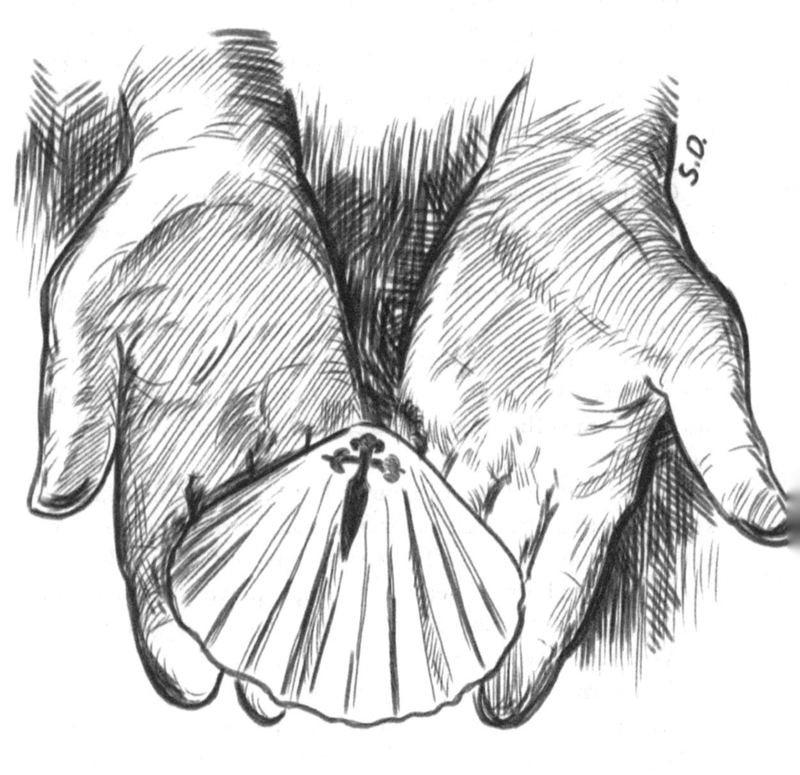

TOMORROW MORNING THE MATH TEACHER AND I shall become pilgrims. We shall travel the breadth and width of Spain, solely on foot. We shall live out of backpacks. We shall be dependent on the charity of strangers whose native tongue we cannot speak without consulting the dark mysticism of Google Translate. We shall be ordering from restaurant menus simply by pointing to the pictures and saying, "I'll have this, *por favor*." We shall be using public Turkish toilets, which, let's be clear about this, are nothing but literal craters in the festering ground.

And I can't believe this is happening. I can't believe my wife and I are doing this.

We are *really* doing this.

I have been up all night packing, scrupulously adding and subtracting to my backpack. It feels weird going overseas with nothing but a backpack. Normally I'd be carrying two carry-ons and one checked suitcase about the size of a minifridge. But all I have is a backpack and my fiddle.

The fiddle is wrapped tightly in a trash bag for waterproofness, then tied with paracord. There is a drinking-water tube snaking from my pack's hydration bladder. My backpack is littered with trinkets for good luck. Most of these were given to me by people who were wishing me well at our farewell supper tonight.

Our last meal in the States was kind of emotional. All our friends came together to wish us luck at a Chinese restaurant. My friend Fred gave me a necklace with a yoga symbol on it. My sister gave me a pin with an astrology sign on it. I think I'm a Capricorn, but I don't remember. My friend Bobby gave me a small rock that was actually a piece of petrified dinosaur dung. Then we all stood in the parking lot and we hugged and hugged. They wished me luck and said they would be praying for me. And I felt much the same way I felt when I first moved away from home. I hugged my mother in the driveway for the last time and knew I was doing something good and wonderful, about to embark on an adventure, but I was also full of tears. That's how it felt last night. Like I was somehow saying goodbye to Old Sean. Welcoming in the new one.

And so now I stand in front of the mirror, wearing a cowboy hat, boots, and hiking shorts. The hat belonged to my father. My fiddle case is secured to my backpack, rising a full eight inches behind my head. My grandfather played fiddle. I used to sit on the porch and watch his adept fingers move across the fingerboard and fall into a daze. I wanted to play music so badly I could taste it. Music somehow became my life at age fourteen. My primary means of eking out a living. I met Jamie, the math teacher, when I was twenty. I played music in places with neon signs in the windows and vomit stains on the stage. On Sundays and Wednesday nights, I played piano at the Baptist church. I am so grateful for Jamie inasmuch as she gave my life direction. Also, because a musician without

a wife or a van is homeless.

"Are you ready?" the math teacher asks, standing in the mirror next to me. She is dressed for bed. She has just finished brushing her teeth with her hiking toothbrush, which I recently cut the handle off of with a hacksaw to save 0.000043 ounces of pack weight. I did this because my wife watched a YouTube video that said all serious hikers cut their toothbrush handles with hacksaws. You don't even want to know what they do with rolls of toilet paper.

"I don't know if I'm ready," I say. "Are you?"

"I think so."

"Are we really doing this?"

"We're really doing this."

"How long will we be out there again?"

"A month and a half."

I am the same age as my father was when he died. I am looking in the mirror at a face that is almost identical to his. I bear my father's likeness. And with the cowboy hat on, I could be his carbon copy.

"We are really doing this?" I say again.

"We are really doing this."

In a few days, we will walk the entirety of Spain, hiking upward of 798 kilometers, over Pyrenees Mountains, on foot, across an entire country. How do you know if you're ready for such things? A lot could happen out there.

The success rate for Camino pilgrims isn't high. Each year, about 543,000 pilgrims start the Camino, and only forty percent finish. According to some books, it's less than twenty percent.

"Tomorrow we will be *real* pilgrims," I say.

"Actually, we're pilgrims as of right now," she says.

She's right. And I've never been a proper pilgrim before. What even *is* a pilgrim? A pilgrim is not just someone who wears a hat shaped like a traffic cone and eats turkey with Squanto and John Smith. A pilgrim is someone who journeys for spiritual reasons. Someone who wanders through a foreign land, looking to be changed. You don't see many pilgrims in modern American society.

Almost every world civilization considers pilgrimages to be of high importance. From archaic and remote tribes, to the most advanced cultures in Asia, Europe, the Middle East, and Africa. Pilgrimages are journeys to visit important things. Pilgrimages are held as transformative life events. But few in modern America care about such events anymore. Instead, we bitch about Cracker Barrel logos and fight in the comment section about whether Mister Rogers was a closet racist. We sit behind desks, working our lives away, receiving our Amazon deliveries, eating our preservative-laced everything, paying our bills like good little consumers, and playing on our phones until our faces go slack from the opiate glow of our phosphorous blue-lit screen.

"We really need to get to bed," my wife says, clicking off

the bathroom light to make her point.

I look at her. Her face is smooth. Her hair pulled back.

"Why are we doing this?" I ask.

Our reasons for hiking the Camino are still a little unclear. What is pulling us toward the path? We are definitely not going just for fun. There is something at work within me that I cannot articulate. Am I searching for myself? Who am I? Have I even found myself?

I think back over the years.

As a kid, I definitely had not found myself yet. I was a chubby boy with corkscrew curly red hair with name tags sewn into all my clothes. Even my underwear had name tags. My mother did this just in case someone attacked me from behind and stole my undergarments. That way, my attacker would never forget where his newly acquired underpants came from.

By my teens, I had definitely not found myself. I was just sad, mostly. I was a loner. I was kind of an orphan. My mother checked out emotionally. I learned how to entertain myself. I usually spent about six hours per day in my room playing an instrument or reading books. Just trying to forget that I was trapped in a life I hated.

In middle school, things got worse. I dropped out. One day I just quit going. And my mother let me because we were white trash. What did it matter? I would not return to my education until decades later. This is the single most mistake I regret. I could have learned so much if I had just kept going to school.

But I didn't. As a result, I had very few friends. And as a result of *that*, I had very few overall interests, save for girls. But girls weren't exactly fawning all over guys who had their names stitched into their underpants. So for many years, I was just one of those faceless tragic teens, trapped in a hormonal body and utterly terrified someone was going to notice him. Or worse, God forbid, *speak* to him.

By my twenties, I was no closer to finding myself than I was to discovering nuclear cold fusion. I worked construction by day and played music by night. I played in bar bands, in rundown joints. Also, I had become a pleaser. A classic try-to-fit-inner. I had always been an outsider, and I just wanted to belong somewhere. In my twenties, I cared deeply about what others thought about me. By my thirties, I was beginning to quit caring what they thought about me. By my forties, I realized nobody had been thinking about me at all.

At no point within this chronology did I find myself. I just sort of—I don't know—kept going. Then—bam!—one morning I was the same age my father was when he removed himself from this world. I never even expected to reach this age. I don't know why. Maybe I thought I didn't deserve the privilege of age.

So that's where I am, as I write this. I'm wondering what I am searching for out there on this far-flung Spanish highway. I don't even know why I'm going. All I know is that my wife and I are drawn to the Camino de Santiago. It is a powerful feeling I have seldom experienced before. Like there is a giant magnet overseas, and the magnet is set to "Sean Mode." There is a yearning for the trail I cannot name.

And so it is, tomorrow morning we will fly into France. We will be deposited in a large airport with nothing but backpacks, water bottles, and walking shoes. We will then take a tiny cab across weaving mountain highways to a tiny farming village where the bulk of the town population is comprised primarily of goats. We will then traverse five hundred miles on foot, starting in Saint-Jean-Pied-de-Port, hiking the length of Spain, trekking across a rugged landscape, over Pyrenees Mountains, through the Galician wilderness, and into Santiago de Compostela, where, if we are among the fortunate, we will die from a heart attack.

"What do you think we'll find out there?" I ask my wife.

"Not sure."

"Then how will we know when we find it?"

"We'll just know, I guess."

She removes my cowboy hat and places it on her own head. Then she kisses me. Then hugs me.

And when she embraces me, something happens. Something real. I feel an overpoweringly familiar feeling sweep over my body. A feeling I haven't felt in many, *many* years. It is a uniquely immersive sensation. A feeling that envelopes my whole physical frame. My whole being. Each organ. Each blood vessel. Each bone. Even my hands and fingers. It's like electricity, almost. Only softer, and more inviting. The sensation I feel is not solely the embrace of my wife. It is as though an abiding and mysterious maternal spirit is hugging me both from the inside as well as the outside. The feeling is akin to being swallowed.

"I've got you," says my wife.

*I*N THE ELEVENTH CENTURY, A GROUP OF SPANISH monks had an idea. They would erect a cross on the highest point of the Camino. It would be a tall cross, reaching 1,504 meters into the sky, situated between Foncebadón and Manjarín, overlooking miles of countryside below. The cross would be made of iron so it could withstand the elements. It would be made tall so that it was visible despite heavy snowfall in the winter. The cross would be a beacon for pilgrims. A marker. A reminder. A signpost. An encouragement. To keep going.

In those days, pilgrims were not mere hikers. They did not have North Face apparel, trail runners, and anti-chaffing powder. They were peasants who had left their jobs, their homes, and their families. They had nothing. They lived on nothing. By the highest point of the Camino, their shoes were gone. Their clothes had become rags. Their feet were bloody. This was the portion of the trail where the going got tough, and the tough died.

There were robbers along this section of trail; there was illness, unforgiving terrain, remote regions, lack of water, lack of food, injury, and good old-fashioned heat exhaustion. And still they had to keep walking. What else could they do? There were no cab services to carry them hundreds of miles back home. No grocery stores. No hostels or municipal albergues with comfy bunk beds. If you'd made it this far, you were in it to win it. You are in it to win it.

Those pilgrims are my ancestors. They are your ancestors. And I'm thinking about those ancestors tonight as our plane flies over the Atlantic.

I'm sitting in an airline seat, staring out a window, thinking about my forebears. Which ones among them felt an attraction to the Camino? And why. They were people who needed miracles but didn't know how to find them. So they just walked. They walked until they received . . .

Well.

Something. Anything.

Imagine what they must have gone through.

You're a farmer in the Middle Ages, 1000 AD-ish. They don't call you a farmer but a *yeoman*, which is an antiquated way of saying "you shovel excrement for a living." Maybe you live in Scotland. Maybe France. England, Portugal, Holland, Sudan, Persia. Wherever. Either way, you have a need. A great need. Maybe your child is ill. Maybe your wife is dying. Maybe you're dying. Or maybe it's something much more elusive than this. Maybe your problem isn't clearly defined.

Maybe you grieve. Maybe you are suicidal. Maybe someone sexually abused you. Maybe your baby died during childbirth. Maybe you're sick. Maybe you just hurt inside and wish there was more to life than what you are experiencing now.

Or maybe your life isn't bad at all. Maybe you have things pretty good, which your people keep reminding you of. Maybe you have wonderful friends, a great family, and a great life. You are even allowed to drink beer for breakfast because this is what yeomen do during the Middle Ages. Even clergymen and toddlers drink beer for breakfast. So that's pretty great.

Perhaps you're mostly okay. You have a good thing going on. Even so, underneath it all there is something happening inside you. You have a need. Centuries later, psychologists will invent clinical names for your feelings. They'll call them "climacteric events" or the "need for self-actualization." They'll say you have "emotional wounds" or that you need "closure."

But in the Middle Ages there are no psychological doctors. There are only doctors whose entire medical practice consists of drilling holes into people's skulls in hopes of curing a runny nose. Your cousin Alfie had that done once. Now, whenever Alfie hears a rooster crow he wets his pants and forgets his name for thirty minutes.

So you can't explain this pulling sensation inside you. It's tugging you somewhere. *Isn't life more than this?* the voice inside keeps saying.

It's not religion you're looking for. Religious people have tried to shove their answers down your throat for years. But they are ceremoniously, and prodigiously, full of crap. Anyone who believes he or she has found the answers is already lost. Only the fool doth think he is wise, whereas a wise man knoweth himself to be a fool.

In other words, this is a spiritual problem. Not a religious one. And, well, you have a few options for spiritual guidance in your century. You could visit your local monastery, but the monks and priests will just instruct you to say twenty-five Hail Marys and call it a day. You could visit the soothsayer, an old local woman with warts on her nose who compels people to drink teas made from substances usually found in barnyards and sheep pens. Likewise, you could visit the town doctor, who just bought a new cordless drill.

But none of this appeals to you.

Then one day you hear about this place in northwestern Spain, hundreds of miles from your home. It's a cathedral, built upon the bones of the apostle James. Furthermore, you've heard that people from all over the world are traveling to this sacred place looking for answers too. Miracles. Rebirth. And people are receiving these things. You heard about a blind man who had his sight restored. A toddler who was healed of a missing limb. Roasted chickens that were raised from the dead.

So immediately, you're thinking, *I must go there!*

The next day you pack your satchel. You tell your wife that you're walking to Spain. Whereupon your wife freaks out. Spain? You're hiking to *Spain*? What the hell, bro?

What about your life? she says. What about your farm? Your family? You can't just leave everything behind. You have bills. You have obligations. You have commitments. You think that annual subscription to Disney Plus pays for itself? Has all that breakfast beer gone to your head?

"But I must go," you insist. "I must walk the Camino de Santiago." You begin weeping as you say it. You don't know why you're crying. The crying takes you by surprise. Where did all these tears come from? You're a yeoman, for crying out loud. Yeomen don't cry.

But this is a pivotal time in your life. You're the same age as your yeofather was when he died. Life is flying past you at a hundred miles per hour, and if you don't do this thing now, you never will.

Your wife sits down with you on the kitchen floor. She holds you. You aren't so much a man right now, in her arms. Your wife gazes into your eyes. She wipes all moisture away.

"Then I'm going with you," your wife says.

The next morning you both leave on foot. You become pilgrims. Your full-time job is now walking. You sleep alongside highways. You eat the food of donations. You brave severe weather. You fend off hypothermia, heat, violence, food poisoning, and whatever else you encounter. You go to bed hungry sometimes. Your feet bleed. Your legs ache. You begin to grow weary. Is whatever you're looking for really worth all this trouble?

I look out the airplane window, asking myself that same question. The Atlantic is miles below. There is a cowboy hat under my seat. A beautiful woman is beside me.

And a smooth stone in my hand.

One thousand years ago, the pilgrims started a tradition. They carried stones in their pockets. The stones represented individual burdens. They represented agony and sorrow. Grief and pain. Bitterness. Resentment. Regret. Loss. Any burden the pilgrim carried, the stone represented it.

The pilgrims of old would carry these stones all the way to Santiago and leave them there, at the gates. Signifying the release from burdens at the gates of heaven. Sadly, many pilgrims did not make it to Santiago. Many pilgrims died on their journey, with stones in their pockets.

So somewhere along the way, pilgrims of yore started leaving their stones at the *Cruz de Ferro*, the highest point on the trail. Who knows why they started doing this. Maybe because many of these peasant pilgrims knew they weren't going to make it. Maybe because they realized it didn't matter whether they made it to Santiago or not, for they had already found what they were seeking.

Maybe they left the stones at the cross because the stones were heavy. All burdens are. Or perhaps the ancient pilgrims understood that nobody was forcing them to carry these stones in the first place. Perhaps they saw clearly that the only one who can release a burden is the one who shoulders it. Nobody can do it for you.

Either way, the mass of stones beneath the iron cross began to grow over the centuries. The pile of rocks and keepsakes grew so big at the cross that the cross seemed to grow shorter each year. The pile would grow so tall that it would flatten itself with gravity. Then it would grow even taller, and wider, until the pile began to resemble a small hillside. Then a small mountain. Then Everest.

The mass of stones still stands. It's enormous, they say. These are the burdens of a thousand years. The burdens come from every corner of the planet. From every era. From each epoch. From every child of God who has ever tread upon this sod. These are their problems. These are their heartaches. Their anguish. Their pain. Their literal tears. And each one of these burdens' owners consciously laid them down.

Most modern-day pilgrims spend the first half of their Camino picking out rocks on the trail to represent their struggles, burdens, and prayers. You have to look for just the right stone, they say. But others bring rocks from home, like me. They carry these rocks on the plane. Try explaining this to the TSA personnel. Other pilgrims bring mementos from their troubled past. Keepsakes from family. Some bring the ashes of loved ones.

I hold the small stone in my hand, thumbing it gently. When you arrive at the cross, you are supposed to leave your rocks and walk away. This is symbolic. And, if I'm being honest, a little cheesy. But everyone does it. So I must join them.

I glance out the airliner window again.

I can't see the ocean. The sky looks eternal, purple and blue and peppered with stars.

Earlier we ate our complimentary airline meal, which tasted like an undercooked athletic supporter. But I didn't care what the food tasted like. I was too lost in my head.

Out the small airplane window I could only see a table of cumulus clouds. A big down quilt, stretched out as far as I could see. The sun was setting. The sky was orange and pink. If I didn't know better, I'd guess I was trapped within the opening credits of *Highway to Heaven* minus the awesome power of Michael Landon's hair.

Now there is a beautiful yeowoman beside me, sleeping soundly. We are wearing the same clothes we will be wearing for almost two months. As I fall asleep, I am thinking how none of this feels real. None of this seems like something I would do. Who am I?

Doesn't matter.

We are really doing this.

11:26 A.M.—WE HAD A FEW TRAVEL MISHAPS WHEN we first arrived in Spain. After our plane touched down in Adolfo-Suarez Madrid-Barajas airport, we were lost for several hours. Namely, because our cellular service provider has screwed up our account somehow and our GPSes now have the same level of cell service as residential refrigerators.

12:38 P.M.—Relying solely on our skills to communicate via fluent hand gestures, we have successfully taken three wrong buses to our destination. The people in this country seem aloof, until you actually talk to them. Then you realize that each one is more friendly than any American I've ever met, except Mister Rogers, who I met when I was six, along with Mister McFeely, the postman.

The good news is, the Spanish I learned on construction jobsites as a young man is coming in handy. The locals love to hear me say "nail gun" in Spanish. They gather around me and say, *"Otra vez,"* which means "Say it again." So I do, and they just laugh and laugh.

The people of Madrid are very genial. Although, evidently, nobody in this country seems to think Mexican swear words are funny.

2:01 P.M.—Evidently my Spanish sucks. Even so, I am actually able to have long conversations with locals provided they talk in a slow, deliberate manner, as though they have just suffered a severe stroke. When locals hear that we are pilgrims walking the Camino, everyone's faces light up, they become reverent, and they treat us as though we are special. I did not expect this kind of reaction. I expected the same reaction a resident in Orlando gives when someone says their kids have always wanted to see Disney World.

Amazingly, spirituality is not a weird or awkward subject for the people of Madrid; it's normal. Here, people seem to treat the topic of religion as cordially as you'd discuss college football. Whereas when you mention religion in America, people edge away from you as though you are a Jehovah's Witness selling Amway.

3:12 P.M.—I found the rooftop at our hostel, which overlooks the city. The view is incredible. Madrid looks like a fairy tale. Houston, we have beer.

4:09 P.M.—Apparently the only Europeans who book stay at hostels are young people. Everyone here looks like they could be twelve years old. We are definitely being treated like elderly persons by our youthful staff of tweens. One extremely young employee asks whether either of us needs our shower to have rails.

6:11 P.M.—We eat supper downtown, approximately eight hours before actual Europeans eat their dinner. We walk a few miles to find a local hot spot recommended by a hostel employee who is not old enough to shave.

The restaurant waitstaff thinks it is cute that Americans are looking for supper at six o'clock. "Sometimes we eat supper at midnight in Spain," the waiter explains.

Still, they serve us delicious gazpacho, which is Spanish for "acid reflux." The food is incredible. They are treating us like we are family. I never want to go home.

1:35 A.M.—Our hostel. There are many of us crammed into one bunkroom. I am on the topmost bunk so that whenever I have to use the restroom in the middle of the night, all the young people in the bunks below me get to enjoy the experience of hearing a grown man descend a wooden ladder that creaks louder than a dump truck ramming into a Steinway plant. I get up to pee six times during the night.

3:43 A.M.—Jet lag is real. I am up before all of Spain, I think. At the least, I am certainly awake hours before my hostel pals, who all just got in a few minutes ago after partying all night like they were at a Who concert. They all collapsed in their bunks and went straight to sleep and will probably sleep until the installation of the next pope. I wish I could do that.

4:10 A.M.—Currently I am on the rooftop with my fiddle, fiddling the tunes "Apple Blossom" and "Redwing" and "Old Fort Smith" with a rubber mute clamped to my violin bridge to kill the sound. Soft melodies of America fill the chilled Spanish air. A few young nightlifers on a nearby rooftop are listening to me. They are smoking strange-smelling cigarettes. They lightly applaud after each tune. They offer me one of the cigarettes, but I tell them I don't smoke. They gather around me, still smoking, and their smoke envelopes my head, and I am coughing. Soon, I see Abraham Lincoln.

The vista is arresting. It's dark. Madrid's rooftop view is nothing but a jigsaw puzzle of terracotta roof tiles and old-school TV antennas for miles.

Even though I said I wasn't going to write while I was here, it's four in the morning and I don't know what else to do. Now and then, I jot a note in my journal about this trip. Then I do a sketch in my Moleskin sketchbook. I've been writing and sketching every morning for almost twelve years now. It started as a blog, but now it's become my life. And I don't know how to stop. In two days, we begin walking the Camino.

6:28 A.M.—Madrid. Our train leaves in an hour and we must hustle. We do not want to miss our train or we will be—how do the Spanish say it?—screwed. We cram clothing into backpacks, leave the hostel, and haul our asses across Madrid to the train station.

7:12 A.M.—We are late arriving at the station. Late by two minutes. We missed our train.

No. This can't be.

7:18 A.M.—We know it's a lost cause, but we still try to get a refund on the tickets because tickets are roughly the same price as a four-bedroom beach condo and I am a writer. "Writer," I am explaining to the guy at the refund desk. "I am a writer. This means I have no money."

The guy at the information desk is very matter-of-fact and says, "No refundos, *señor*. This is Spain, not Walmart."

7:34 A.M.—We purchase new, more expensive tickets for a later train. It's pricey. But it's all right, we can always just get a second mortgage.

To kill time before our departure, we hang out in the station café, drinking coffee. The eatery is full. People are staring at us. This could be because we are the only ones carrying hiking backpacks and a fiddle. Or it might be because I am wearing a cowboy hat, and you don't see many Roy Rogers wannabes in Spain.

One little boy asks me in broken English whether I am a real *vaquero*. I tell him that, yes, Kemosabe, I am most definitely a real *vaquero*, and I have a Lone Ranger lunchbox at home to prove it.

9:36 A.M.—Our train is on time. We rush through security, placing our bags in the scanners. Train security is high today. Locals have told me there is civil unrest in Spain and terrorist organizations usually target transportation hubs. Especially around holidays. It is nearing Easter, which is a MAJOR holiday in Spain. And they really hate Americans.

Goodie, goodie.

Still, even with heightened security, Spanish transportation security agents are polite, quick, and efficient. They do not seem bothered by the fact that we're Americans. They laugh at my jokes. They smile at me a lot. This is a stark contrast to American TSA agents, many of whom seem to be suffering clinical depression.

10:29 A.M.—I am contemplating selling one of my kidneys to pay for the tickets for our next train. We have a layover in Zaragoza, and nobody speaks English here. Thankfully, my Spanish is improving; it's all coming back to me.

I am speaking fluently, feeling pretty good about myself, asking for information from a railway employee on where exactly to stand in line.

The employee begins to chuckle and tells me that I have just asked him, in perfect *Español,* how to remove a bone from the butt of a fire hydrant.

11:48 A.M.—There was an administrative mix-up when the employee booked our tickets. My seat is not located near my wife's. I am sitting in the back of the train, next to a teenage girl who is doing schoolwork on an iPad.

Jet lag is catching up with me. I drift in and out of sleep as our train whirls past miles of farmland and impossibly green mountain pastures.

When I wake up, I see that I've been drooling on myself. The teenage girl finds this amusing and points to my shirt collar, which is wet. I am humiliated, so I apologize and try to explain "jet lag" to her in Spanish, but I don't know how to say this term.

So I attempt to drive my point home by using hand gestures and mouth noises that illustrate a tiny jet flying through the air. The girl looks frightened now. You can see her mind racing, wondering, (a) why is this man using the international hand signs for "airplane"? and (b) is this man a terrorist targeting a major transportation hub?

1:28 P.M.—Our train arrives in Pamplona. It's Palm Sunday. Everyone is happy and in their church clothes. We find a cabdriver willing to carry us to the *Camino Frances* trailhead in

Saint-Jean, where we will register with the Pilgrim's office and begin our walk. The driver speaks no English, but I assure him this is okay because I am very skilled at removing bones from the backsides of fire hydrants.

Before we enter the cab, my wife and I are both drinking coffee from paper cups, but the driver sternly informs us that no coffee is allowed in his cab. We must throw the coffees away right now or he is going to leave us here. I toss the coffee into the air, but a wind gust blows it back toward us. Coffee goes all over the driver. He is not happy.

1:47 P.M.—Driving. Our cab drives along a series of winding roads so intense and curvy that I feel as though I am at Six Flags Over Hell. The twisty roads get worse. The cabdriver tells me I am white as a ghost, and he seems sort of amused by this. I feel like I am going to ralph.

2:01 P.M.—I am ralphing.

Well, at least I am doubled over on the shoulder, dry heaving. My wife rubs my back as our cabdriver says in Spanish, "Now you understand why we don't allow coffee in the cab."

2:45 P.M.— I am sick as a dog, riding in the back seat. Moaning. My wife is up front, teaching our driver how to pronounce American cuss words.

3:08 P.M.—Saint-Jean-Pie-de-Port is a cute, historic French village whose name means, literally, "four hyphens." The village is entirely overrun with pilgrims of all nations, all clad in outdoor activewear. It feels as though we have crawled into an

REI advertisement.

The inn where we are staying is manned (womaned?) by two French women who speak no English and almost no Spanish. Attached to the inn is a little café, which is quaint, smells like bread, and is about the size of a medium-sized bathtub. The two women are furiously buzzing to and fro, preparing orders, trying their best to serve pilgrims, none of whom seem to speak their native tongue.

Some pilgrims are impatient. Most of these impatient pilgrims are American. Many of them are what you might call Karens.

One such American, an older woman, walks into the café and is frustrated because she is unable to find "ranch dressing" on the menu. The American woman gets angry and slams her menu down and finally says, "You REALLY need to learn to speak English in this place." And she leaves.

The French women are cheerfully unbothered by the woman's display.

"Is okay," the happy French woman says to me. "Americans are sometimes—how you say? —jerks." My wife laughs. Then she teaches the French women a new and more anatomical word for "jerk."

5:38 P.M.—Church bells ring across the mountainside. There are sheep grazing in distant pastures. We eat an early supper we got from the market, sitting on a bench overlooking a verdant alpine river gorge. We are eating salads with lots of fresh vegetables that were grown in this village, the woman at the grocery store told us. The tomatoes taste like heaven. Why don't we have vegetables like this back home? Why do our tomatoes taste like sour tennis balls? I have a feeling that, simply by being in Spain, I am about to learn a lot about America.

There is electricity in the air I can't describe. The whole town is humming with unique energy. Thousands of pilgrims are arriving in Saint-Jean, registering to hike the Camino. People are jacked. Everyone is seeking something. Everyone has their reason for walking. I wonder what mine is.

We begin our walk in one day.

SAINT-JEAN-PIE-DE-PORT, FRANCE
MONDAY, APRIL 14, 2025

3:03 A.M.—I'M AWAKE BEFORE MY WIFE. JET LAG HAS ME five kinds of screwed up. It's three in the morning here but 8 p.m. in Alabama.

Thus, I am locked away in our inn's bathroom, door closed, sitting on a latrine, playing my fiddle with the brass mute affixed to the instrument's bridge. Brass mutes eliminate the sound more aggressively than rubber mutes, for those of you who were wondering.

4:10 A.M.—Jamie is still sleeping. I'm still fiddling.

5:37 A.M.—I am now sitting in the inn's garden, fiddling. Sleeping Beauty still hasn't budged. It's dark outside. There are sheep behind me, very interested in what I'm doing. I think they want to eat my fiddle.

There is an older woman in the cottage next door listening to me play through an open window as she works in her kitchen. She pauses to lean out the window and give light applause when I finish playing "Over the Waves." I'm not sure whether she applauded because she liked the song or because I am no longer playing.

6:24 A.M.—I am watching a calico cat creep along terracotta rooftops in the dark distance. He carefully leaps from one roofline to the next. I think he hears my fiddle and is looking for his wounded sibling.

7:28 A.M.—The sun rises in San-Jean-Pie-de-Port, slowly ascending behind the small French hamlet nestled deep within the Pyrenees. Silver mist clings to the mountainsides like a damp dishrag. Distant sheep graze on swatches of green farmland quilting the rocky hillsides. Giving me a kind of hope I cannot fully describe in words. But I will try. It is my great hope that my wife wakes up someday soon.

8:32 A.M.—Jamie is awake. We eat a muesli breakfast, which is cereal that doesn't taste like cereal. It's like oatmeal on steroids, with lots of fresh fruit and nuts, made with apple juice instead of water. It is delicious. Why don't we eat muesli in the US?

Our innkeeper tells us muesli will help us go to the bathroom. The French woman doesn't speak English, so instead of saying "bathroom," she uses gestures to pantomime "severe gastrointestinal distress." Then she laughs. The French are wonderful.

10:00 A.M.—We are at the supermarket, buying food for our upcoming walk. There is evidently no peanut butter in this store, or in all of France. And when you ask any of the French for peanut butter, they act as though you are interested in purchasing a jar of warm sputum.

Also, they sell items in this store I've never heard of. Tiny octopi in a jar. They sell all manner of eggs from various creatures, including the eggs of snails. I didn't know snails even laid eggs.

There are two aisles wholly dedicated to cheese.

In the meat department I see a butcher handling an animal tongue the size of a small toddler. He presents the tongue to an elderly woman who cheers for the slab of muscular organ meat like you'd cheer for a birthday cake.

10:13 A.M.—A supermarket employee informs me that peanut butter is something only Americans eat. The employee cannot even utter "peanut butter" without gagging. He says the French would never eat peanut butter unless they were in a survival situation and cannibalism was no longer a viable option. I tell him that is all well and good, but beef tongues the size of Fiats don't exactly blow my American skirt up either.

12:11 A.M.—The whole town shuts down for two hours. All shops close. Even big, franchise-looking stores and gas stations.

"What do you mean you do not have a two-hour lunch in America?" one shopkeeper asks me amusedly. "Don't you ever take a rest?"

I tell him no, in America we only have sixty-five-hour workweeks and angina. He seems genuinely saddened by this news. But I tell him to look on the bright side, at least we have peanut butter.

2:05 P.M.—We are standing in a *long* line outside the Pilgrim's Office to get our "credentials," which are passports used for the Camino. You need these passport booklets otherwise you cannot stay at the hostels, and we do not plan on sleeping in a pasture where they harvest cow tongue.

There are hundreds of pilgrims in line with us. The line stretches backward, almost to the end of town. Very few pilgrims speak English. We are all from different countries, age groups, and walks of life. And yet, somehow, although we are foreigners sojourning in a strange land, we all manage—this is beautiful—to gripe about how slow the line moves.

Our collective grumbling leads to new friendships. I make friends with an older French man named Lauren, which he pronounces "Law." I try saying his name, but the man tells me I speak bad French and to never try speaking French again if I want to maintain my dignity as a human being.

Also, I meet a German man named Heinrich who only knows one English word, which is *brilliant*, which he uses after everything I say. You could say the sky is fuchsia and the ocean is made of manure and Captain Crunch is the new pope, and Heinrich would smile and gaily reply, "Brilliant."

I meet a twenty-five-year-old Dutch woman who is walking the Camino after a breakup. A forty-six-year-old Vietnamese man who says God told him to walk this path in a dream after his mother died. A twenty-two-year-old guy named Roger from Michigan, who is fervently praying to meet hot girls.

7:08 P.M.— After supper, we are invited to attend a pilgrim's mass at Notre-Dame du Bout du Pont. The ancient church is mostly empty except for a few dozen pilgrims.

Everyone is reverent. Praying up for their walk. A lot of people are bowing their heads. Some light candles. There is a strong sense of joy in the air. It's the same feeling I used to get before Little League games, minus all the chest-slamming. We know we're about to do something that matters. Something big. And we're ready.

An official-looking elderly woman is walking from pew to pew to inform people there will be no Mass tonight for some reason. Even so, this does not stop the horde of pilgrims from genuflecting. We have come a long way to do this. To be here. To feel what we're feeling in this sanctuary. So we continue praying. Some are weeping. I feel a lot of peace.

I unfold the prayer bench and kneel.

I don't know what I'm praying for, exactly, but I begin to weep too. Big tears. I don't know why. Maybe because this all feels so real now. This room. This atmosphere, so heavy with the feeling that we are all looking for something, and we are about to find it.

8:04 P.M.— I finally find peanut butter.

WE LEAVE OUR INN AT DAYBREAK. OUR INN-keeper is awake and already at the front door, wearing a robe, waiting to say goodbye to us. Like a mom seeing her kids off to school. She gives us a heart-felt and emotional goodbye in French, with double kisses and everything.

"*Dieu sout avec toi,*" she says.

I don't speak French, so I answer, "Ten four."

Which she evidently doesn't understand. And there's no way to explain such a philosophical concept as ten four, so I give her a hug instead. The French, I am pleased to learn, are huggers.

And we're off.

Jamie and I are wearing heavy packs. But not as heavy as some pilgrims. Some hikers have fallen victim to overkill pack-ing. They are wearing packs the size of V8 engine blocks. But they will learn. Just like we all will. The first lesson of the Camino, as in life: it is not how much you carry that matters, but how much you are able to leave behind.

There are a handful of other pilgrims leaving San-Jean-Pie-du-Port at the same time we are, making their exodus on foot.

Soon we are all on a highway that winds through impossi-bly green hills. A thick fog drapes itself over the earth. Sheep everywhere. Some of which stand directly in the road and poop while staring at you.

But this is all part of the experience. The fog, the livestock, the poop. Just like life.

I am smoking a short Cuban cigar. You cannot buy Cuban cigars in the US, but you can buy Cubans in France. Cubans make average US cigars taste similar to something sheep leave in roadways. There are other pilgrims, both male and female, also smoking cigars in the spirit of celebrating our first day of walking. The older pilgrims don't mind the cigar smoke. Several younger pilgrims, however, speed around us, fanning the air and pretending to cough.

And so, we walk.

All day.

When you close your eyes, all you hear are the patter of your own footsteps. Occasionally you will pass other pilgrims.

Soon we are all climbing steep mountain highways. And it's all starting to sink in. This is not a "vacation." This is not supposed to be "fun" in the traditional sense of the word. Not unless your idea of fun is receiving an unanesthetized root canal.

Furthermore, we are strangers in this land. This country is

not ours. We are foreigners in a new world. We are outsiders. Pilgrims. We have no home. We are possession-less, except for our packs. We have no family except for each other. And worse, we have no beer. This walk is going to be an allegory for our own lives. You walk. You get blisters. The end. The meaning of life is to give life meaning.

We hike uphill for most of the day until we arrive at our first hostel. We are all a little surprised when the hostel materializes out of the fog like a mirage in the middle of the Pyrenees. Although we cannot see the mountains because the fog is too heavy.

They have food and warmth inside. It looks like an old hunting lodge. The owners are loud and cheerful and very French. The common area is dimly lit and feels more like the convivial atmosphere of a pub. Pilgrims laughing. Glasses clinking. The scent of garlic and shallots fills the air. Fresh baked baguettes. And body odor.

We find our bed is in a bunk room with eight other pilgrims. One of whom is already out like a light and snoring so loud I can feel the vibrations in my dental fillings. Our shower is coin-operated and only runs for three minutes. Three. Also, it's cold water. Deal with it, the staff tells us. In French, of course.

There is no heater in our bunk room. Everyone's collective B.O. lends the room the aroma of a giant human gluteal crevice. More pilgrims have gone to bed even though it's daylight outside. Their collective snoring is so loud I am concerned about sleeping tonight.

But this is the Camino.

Supper is a huge deal. Everyone is famished. When the bell rings, pilgrims run—actually run—to the mess hall. The meal features a long table with forty-odd pilgrims and pints of tepid beer. In any other travel scenario, I would have more than enough to complain about. But right now I am just grateful not to be walking.

We pilgrims are told by the innkeepers that before we eat we must stand and introduce ourselves, explaining our reasons for walking.

Most of the pilgrims speak French, Spanish, German, Dutch, Taiwanese, Korean, or something else. English is spoken too, but not much of it. Which makes each English-spoken sentiment seem so incredibly poignant.

"I first walk the Camino many years ago," says one Italian man, "and I was so lonely, so I prayed that I'd find an amazing wife someday." Then he motions to a blushing woman beside him. "This is that amazing wife God give to me, many years ago."

Everyone applauds.

"We walk this trail to thank God for the gift of each other, and for the gift of love."

The applause is even louder this time.

A French woman says, "I walk this Camino because I need to find my spirit again. I am lost. I do not know who I am anymore. I have been so long identifying with my husband, and now that he is gone, I am in need of finding me again."

Applause again.

An older Taiwanese guy: "I believe I am here to rediscover my life and my soul."

A young Austrian woman: "I walk so I won't waste my life."

A man with a Tennessee accent: "I want to find God. I know he's there, but I keep missing him."

More applause.

Throughout the night there is much laughter around our table, and much wine. There is not a single shallow conversation among us. No insincere formalities. No insecure one-upmanship games. This is not meaningless cocktail party talk. ("So, how strong is your investment portfolio, Chaz?")

No. Tonight people are talking about real things. They speak of God, and love, and Grace, and Peace, and fear, and sorrow, and Christ, and forgiveness, without apprehension or worry about a mixed audience. They speak of the many faults of man-made religion, the lifelong, bone-crushing search to find out who we are, why we have the capacity to suffer, and why, most of all, we choose to walk this road. We discover how similar we all are. Which is both comforting and eerie at the same time. These are people from different countries, but we feel related somehow.

New friendships are made. New resolutions are formed. New journeys begin. Prayers are uttered. You can feel something happening here.

And soon it's time to visit the bunk room to see which one of us snores the loudest.

Please, God, don't let it be me.

WE START PREPARING TO WALK TO SANTIAGO before sunrise. Pilgrims are lacing up boots in the darkness outside our hostel. Many languages are spoken this morning. Many, *many* languages. But no English.

I see patches of snow outside. It's cold in these mountains. And windy. And I'm just trying to keep to myself because I don't understand anything anyone is saying.

Then a guy sits beside me.

"This seat taken?" he says. He has a Southern accent.

"It is now," I say.

He smiles. "Hey, your accent. You from Georgia?"

"Alabama."

"Close enough."

"Not by SEC standards, it isn't."

His name is Steve, but we all call him Chattanooga. That's how it works out here. Nobody has used my name on the Camino so far. They all call me Alabama.

Chattanooga and I shake hands. He and I are so grateful to have someone we can speak English with that we are talking a blue streak. It's really quite novel, meeting another Southerner in this far-off nation. And it feels doubly weird to speak about American things in this setting. All those things seem almost surreal as we stare at the Pyrenees.

"Isn't this *freaking* amazing?" Chattanooga says. "To be in a place where you don't know anyone and yet you feel so close to everybody?"

"It really is."

"I would've never guessed this was how it would go."

He's right. It is strange. To feel deep comradeship with to-tal foreigners. People you might otherwise never interact with. Normally you wouldn't even talk to these people. And they wouldn't talk to you. They wouldn't have a reason to. You would stay in your own bubbles. But you're speaking now. In fact, you do more than speak. You empathize.

Breakfast is light. Steve has Cornflakes. I have coffee. I'm trying to coax my muscles into a second day of abuse. An older Korean man at the table sees my cowboy hat and is intrigued. He asks to try on the hat, communicating with gestures.

"Hat? Hat?" he is saying.

I take off the hat and give it to him.

He places the ten-gallon lid on his head. The headwear is four sizes too big, drooping on his head like Speedy Gonzalez's sombrero, but he is elated. The man poses for multiple

pictures with his friends, holding pretend air-pistols, saying to the camera, "I am *Crint Eastrood.*"

The Korean men are old high school friends. They are walking the path to celebrate forty years of friendship. He hands the hat back and God-blesses me.

Our walk begins.

The sun is not yet up. Pilgrims are on the desolate highway, trudging onward in the dark of morning. We are in the deep hills. There are no houses out here. No barns. No evidence of man. Just lots of livestock, all held captive without fences. Because where would they go?

It's foggy; we can't see anything except our own feet. But then the sun comes up. Sunrise starts slow, then intensifies. Like the second movement of a symphony. That's when we realize we are in the real Pyrenees. Not a reasonable facsimile of the Pyrenees. Not a tourist-bred imitation of mountains. We're in the actual Pyrenees. It looks like we are walking through a foreboding Shangri-La. There is snow on the ground in some places. The wind is so intense it stings my face. And the wind is picking up speed.

"This wind is horrible!" shouts my wife over the sound of the wind.

"Don't walk too close to the edge!"

All morning Jamie and I hike. We aren't talking. We're together, technically, but alone in our thoughts. Everyone hikes the Camino alone, sort of. Even when you're with your people, you're always alone. Alone with your thoughts. You do not belong to an organized hiking party with a guide. There are no paid lunches and informational lectures with a group. Out here it's just you. Just the road.

We are climbing ginormous hills, surrounded only by towering granite slabs and the occasional herd of horses. The fog behind us finally settles in mountain valleys like suds in a bathtub.

We are walking a steep incline now. We are leaning forward and breathing heavily with each step. Then the wind picks up again. And by "picks up," I mean the gusts become strong enough to knock pilgrims off their feet. We meet at least six older hikers who are forced to quit the trail after injuries caused by falls due to wind. The gusts are sometimes so intense you can hardly open your eyes.

We pass many pilgrims taking shelter against massive rocks, waiting for the gusts to die down. We wave at them as we pass. Some of them look pretty beat-up.

Then a bitingly cold alpine tempest sweeps up and almost knocks me off my feet. I somehow maintain my balance. Jamie and are shouting to be heard over the gale.

"We need to get out of this wind!"

"I'm so cold!"

"I can't feel my hands!"

"Where can we take shelter!?"

"There is nowhere!"

So we keep walking. What other option is there?

We are now leaning so hard into the headwind, to prevent falling backward onto our fat American aspirations, that our noses are almost touching the pavement. This is all beginning to feel dangerous now. One wrong fall and you could tumble down a mountainside. This was definitely not in the brochures.

Then we see it.

There ahead, in the fold of the craggy rocks, sits another group of pilgrims, huddled together, taking shelter. Alex and Eric and Christina. They were at our hostel last night. We join them. We are all breathless and panting from exhaustion. We are windburned and ready to quit for the day, but we have barely begun.

"I've never seen wind like this," says Alex, who is an English teacher from Argentina.

"Someone could really get hurt out there," says Christina, who's from the Netherlands.

My hat keeps blowing off, so I try several different ways of securing it to my head. Nothing works; it keeps getting caught by the gale. I find baling wire in the mud beneath my feet, not far from a small section of wire fencing. I thread the wire through vent holes in the hat and fashion a chinstrap.

Eventually, we all decide to brave the wind together. We five unlikely pilgrims leave the security of our cleft, and soon we are climbing forbidden slopes again, wading through mud, marching across sheep pastures, plodding into titanic piles of fresh livestock offerings.

After hiking all day, we reach Roncesvalles. The town is known for its former-monastery-turned-hostel. Most pilgrims are stopping here for the night. The pilgrims have had enough abuse for one day. They're tired and hungry. Everyone's skin is red from the wind. Everyone's hair looks like they recently licked an electrical socket. The monastery is a popular stop on the route, and now we know why.

Exhaustion.

The monastery is huge, made of stone, built in 1132 AD, with all the warmth and charm of a federal prison. There are pilgrims outside, dressed in lounge clothes, who all look about as happy as inmates on strip-search day. They are chain-smoking and not talking. You can see their thoughts written on their faces. They are thinking, *We have to walk five hundred miles of this?*

I see Chattanooga; he's sitting on a stone, massaging his knee. His face is contorted with pain.

"What's wrong?" I ask.

"I don't know," he says. "I've never had knee problems in my life, but all of a sudden, my knee hurts."

He experiments with a few knee positions and winces. "I've done something to it," he says. "Something bad."

Meanwhile, everyone is talking about the wind and how they almost didn't make it. There are undertones of doubt within everyone's voices. Everyone is having second thoughts. Everyone is saying they didn't know it would be this hard.

Jamie and I decide not to stay at the monastery-slash-correctional-facility. There is too much negativity in the air. If we stay, we might get infected with it.

We bid everyone goodbye and keep walking. We press on toward the next town. Christina decides to join us. She does not mind the smell of the cigar. She says it reminds her of her dad.

So there is hope for this world after all.

We are on the road for hours. Alone again. Alone together.

Nobody is talking. We are serenaded only by the crunching of our own feet in the snow. Soon the wind picks up again. My Stetson is catching gusts like the mainsail of a yacht. Soon our backs hurt. Our butts hurt. Our hips hurt. We are cold. We are tired. Slightly sunburned. Confused. And underneath it all there is a strange and unusual joy set before us. On our way, we pass a highway sign that reads SANTIAGO—790 KILOME-TERS.

"Oh hell," says my wife.

"Seriously?" says Christina.

"*Sí*," says Crint Eastrood."

W E HAVE NO ROOMS," THE INNKEEPER SAYS over the phone.

"None?" I ask.

"We are full, *señor*."

My wife and I are sitting on the ancient steps of a very old church in Puenta la Reina. We are dusty and sweaty, and one of us smells like a giant armpit. (*Moi.*) The stone doorway arch above us features carvings of angels and demons, relief carvings that date back to Roman times. Eight angels surround the risen Christ, who is looking straight at me as though he is saying, "No room at the inn? Now where have I heard *that* before?"

"Please," I say to the innkeeper. "There are no rooms anywhere; we will sleep on the floor if we have to."

"I said *no room*." And the woman hangs up.

I stare at my phone for a few moments.

"She hung up on me," I say.

"What're we gonna do?" my wife asks.

I shake my head. "She actually hung up on me."

It is late siesta in Spain. No traffic on the highways. No pilgrims we can see on the Camino de Santiago. The streets are vacant. Most pilgrims have already found lodging for the evening and are already receiving their complimentary massages and mimosas.

At least that's what I imagine. Because we have been hunting for a room all day, and there are no vacancies for another twenty miles.

It is Holy Week, which is the biggest holiday week in Spain. It's like the Superbowl, the National Championship, Mardi Gras, Christmas, Thanksgiving, Fourth of July combined. I had no idea how big this celebration was. The locals all return to their hometowns. They come from the four corners of the earth. The airlines and train stations are flooded to the point of collapse. Small villages are clogged with people, lined with thousands of cars, parked on the side of the road. There are parades. Villages come together and shoot cannons and fireworks, and beat gigantic drums that can be heard for miles. And they eat until they puke. Literally. This is an ancient Roman tradition, I am told, to eat until you must induce vomiting, then it is customary to return back inside and eat some more. I am not making this up. We have nothing in the US that is even remotely like *Semana Santa* in Spain.

As a result, there are more hikers on the Camino right now then there have been in many years, according to one innkeeper. He's never seen so many *peregrinos*, not in fifty years of service. We pilgrims have jammed up this country by the hundreds of thousands. Finding a room in Spain is like trying to locate a porta john at a bluegrass festival.

I am still staring at the call-ended screen.

"She hung up on me," I say in disbelief.

This is not good. All day we have been hearing about pilgrims turned away from hostels. Some, we learn, have been forced to sleep outside on doorsteps. Some pilgrims are sleeping on the stoops of churches. Today I met a group of pilgrims who all slept in a pasture, using backpacks for pillows, huddled together for warmth. They started a campfire out of—again, I am being serious—dried sheep dung.

"Sheep dung burn really good," said the Korean kid who lit the fire.

This is not the Camino I dreamed of.

I put my phone away and take a moment.

I need to get my head together. I need to figure out what we should do. Otherwise, we're sleeping outside tonight. And I really don't want to know what flaming ram excrement smells like.

I wander into the church while Jamie sits on the steps watching our backpacks.

I cross myself and take a pew.

There are people praying in this chapel. They look like locals, not pilgrims. Tomorrow is Good Friday, and the town has come out to offer thanks for their families, to light candles and say prayers.

And I am looking at a sculpture of Christ on a cross. I am lost in a daze, staring at this ornate altar. I see a woman and her child approach the votives and insert coins into a box. They light several candles, then kneel to pray to the crucifix.

I find myself thinking about what it truly means to truly be executed by crucifixion. I don't know why these thoughts are filling my head.

Perhaps because my entire evangelical childhood featured gratuitous amounts of imagery of the crucifixion. We sang cute little Sunday school songs about nails and crowns of thorns. We wore tiny crucifixes around our necks. We had paintings and sculptures portraying the crucifixion. Jesus always had great abs.

You grow up seeing this scene so many times, you become numb to the idea of a human being being nailed to a cross like meat. It loses all impact. But right now, in light of *Viernes Santo*, as I sit in this chapel, I'm thinking about it differently.

First, you're stripped nude.

You are not a fitness model with defined abdominal muscles. You are a thirty-something male who eats a lot of bread and drinks wine with every meal. And it shows in your midsection. You are embarrassed. You are naked in front of everyone.

You are then taken away by your captors, still naked. You are made a display for the town to see. You are a sideshow.

You are exposed to everyone. They can all see your bareness. They see your anatomy. Then a crowd of onlookers watches as a group of eighteen-year-old soldiers with egos to prove kicks the proverbial stew out of you. Next, they place you on timbers. They mutilate your hands with nails. Romans didn't always use just one nail per hand. Sometimes they used three or four, until the bones of the hand were obliterated.

Then you just hang there.

It's not beautiful. It's not art. It's gross. It's raw. There are no orchestras playing overtures. No cinematic key lighting. Your cross stands erected on Main Street, in the sunshine. Your basic human reflex is to shield your nudity. But you can't. Sometimes you have to go to the bathroom. So you just do. You are crucified alongside dozens of others, usually. Thus, the streets are bathed in urine from other crucifixion victims.

The boy-soldiers beneath your cross are horsing around, engaging in locker room banter, shooting craps, seeing which one will win your shoes.

Soon you can't breathe.

Now your lips are turning blue.

Your arms are numb.

Your serratus muscles and shoulders are tearing from struggling against your own body weight. You feel your back muscles ripping. You feel your shoulders dislocating. Your wrists pop. Your hands are tearing beneath your bodyweight.

You're thirsty.

They give you a sponge, soaked in vinegar.

And the worst part is, almost none of your friends are here. Few are brave enough to attend your last hours. Doesn't anyone care about you? Isn't anyone going to show their love to you? Isn't anyone going to look at you and say, "I'm here"? Aren't you important in anyone's life?

Meantime, there are four other guys crucified alongside you. Hollywood films and various evangelical bumper stickers will depict only three crosses on this fateful Friday. But some scholars say there are five crosses, maybe more, and you're just one of them. Meaning, you are just a guy in this crowd of thieves and criminals. You are not world famous. You are not given special treatment. No sacred ceremony. You are just another state inmate on the roadside.

No big deal.

It's people who did this to you. People. Not wild animals. Not an act of nature. Fellow human beings. Because the harsh truth is, people are not always nice. People are mean. People hate. People start wars. People mutilate animals in the name of fashion and wipe out entire species. People obliterate a continent's native tribes, strip-mine the soil, and cut down miles of trees, only to erect a Starbucks in their place. People posture, they compete, they kill. They invent rules and dogmas simply to exclude others.

And in your moment of nude agony, in your moment of sorrow, in your moment of death, you see all these failings of human nature beneath you. You watch it all, with your human eyes. You are alone without friends.

And you forgive them. For we know not what we do.

I cross myself and exit the chapel.

My wife is sitting on the steps with our bags. We still have no room to speak of. We are low on food. I am thirsty, but I'll live. We have a long way to Santiago. But tomorrow is Good Friday. And I think, perhaps, I am figuring out why I'm walking.

ODAY IS GOOD FRIDAY. *VIERNES SANTO.* AND MY mood has fallen. We started this walk excited. We started this walk majorly pumped. But as each day goes by, we are becoming more crestfallen and disappointed. Each day, we continue to learn more and more that *Semana Santa* in Spain is no joke. Each day, we are reminded of how this country is in full-on party mode, and how there are no lodgings, and how if there ever *are* any available overnight accommodations, they are for livestock and the living space's main feature is a manger.

And now that it's almost Easter Sunday, things have amped up. We pilgrims have all been as beggars, compelled to walk with hats in hand, our hands out, constantly looking for beds. *"Puede ayudarnos?"* ("Can you help us?") is a phrase I've grown familiar with, asking complete strangers. Usually they shake their heads at me. More pilgrims are growing discouraged and abandoning the trail.

To celebrate the holiday festivities, television stations are broadcasting all the Holy Week classics in *Español. Spartacus, The Silver Chalice, Ten Commandments.* There are decorations. There are street processions, large parades, occurring in almost every little town. These are like minor Bourbon Street celebrations, with Macy's-style floats, people wearing pointy hats, and large statues of different saints, hoisted on the shoulders of many locals who cannot walk in a straight line and keep banging St. Bernadine into various walls and laughing. It's amazing how many people turn out for these parades. I've never seen so many people in one place.

Today's parade, *La Madrugá*, is known as a somber parade wherein people dress up in costumes identical to Ku Klux Klan getups. They promenade down main streets in ornate floats, wearing deathly serious expressions, moving slowly, banging drums, and just generally terrifying the dog doo out of all Americans within eyeshot. But the parade-going crowd isn't serious at all. They are giddy. Their kids are running around, laughing and eating snacks. The atmosphere is anything but somber. It feels like Saint Patrick's Day in Chicago.

Right now I am sitting in a Spanish bar in the dusty pueblo of Villa de Larraga. Villa de Larraga is an infinitesimally small town with stone streets and a bell tower. There are no restaurants. No stores. No nothing. Only a hotel. And one bar. This is evidently a locals' bar. And I believe I am the only *Inglés* speaker in the village tonight.

"*Una cerveza?*" the lady bartender asks. She is older, white-haired, with green eyes.

"*Por favor,*" I reply.

A TV in the corner plays *Ben Hur* at a loud volume, over-dubbed in Spanish. Charlton Heston is in his prime. Everyone in the joint, both young and old, is watching. It is almost comical to watch his mouth as he speaks and hear mismatched rapid-fire Spanish come through the television speakers.

Villa de Larraga is gearing up for a parade tonight. A big one. You can feel it. The whole town is buzzing. Kids play *fútbol* in the streets. Old men sit on benches, sipping wine and smoking cigars. Older women congregate in clumps, talking with violently animated hand movements. We are twenty miles south of the Camino. A long way off course. Our Camino journey is quickly turning into a veritable disaster.

How did we get here? We are here because there are no places to stay near the Camino. Tonight my wife and I found ourselves on another set of doorsteps. We managed to find a place to lay our heads last night, but this time we came scarily close to sleeping on the stairs. We had selected the perfect doorstep for the evening when a taxi driver happened upon us. He saw us on the church stoop and had mercy upon us.

The man pulled over and helped me find a room. We had to search miles out of the way to find one. I must've called six hundred hostels and hotels looking for a vacancy. The only responses I got were *"Completo," "Lleva,"* and *"No hay camas."* All full.

Thanks for playing.

As middle-aged pilgrims on the Camino, my wife and I already accepted that we would be sleeping in some unsavory places. But I didn't think I would actually wind up outside.

The kindly local cabdriver had no reason to help us, but he did. There was nothing in it for him. And yet he took forty-five minutes out of his family holiday to make phone calls, scare us up a room, and then give us a ride, twenty minutes opposite from his direction.

During our cab ride, I think I figured out why he helped us. It was more than him being a nice guy. A lot more. To him, we are pilgrims. And in Spain, they do not treat pilgrims like lowly tourists. Pilgrims are seekers. All who walk the Camino are held with reverential respect. You can see it in the faces of older locals; when you tell them you are walking to Santiago, they take you seriously.

"*Dios, te bendiga*," many of them reply in a tone of profound reverence. Which is Spanish for "God bless you." Sometimes they nod their heads at you and say, "*Vaya con Dios, peregrino.*" ("Go with God, pilgrim.") In their eyes, if you are walking to Santiago, you are doing something of cosmic importance. This is holy business to them. And many feel it is their duty to help you.

So, here I am. Homeless in Spain. And I am rethinking our decision to walk this long path across this country. We have no guarantee of a bed or shelter for the weeks ahead. We have no plans, no arrangements, no lodging reservations. Right now I am feeling foolish. I feel ashamed. I feel stupid. I should've planned better. I should've done something different. I should've . . .

The older woman bartender comes to me and speaks in Spanish. "You are here to watch parade, no?" she says.

"No," I reply in high school *Español.* "Well, I mean, yes. Sort of."

She looks at me quizzically.

She can tell I am crabby, sunburned, and exhausted. "We don't usually get *Americanos* in our village. This is why I ask you this question."

"The reason I'm here is because everywhere else is full."

I gently spin my beer glass in its condensation ring.

"Everywhere?" she says.

"Everywhere," I say with a nod.

And it's no exaggeration. I literally walked the streets of Spain like a vagrant, empty-handed, requesting for help from complete strangers, looking for a room.

"I feel kind of ashamed," I add. "I never should have come to Spain during Holy Week. I had no idea *Semana Santa* was such a big deal."

"You no have *Semana Santa* in America?"

"No."

"No Holy Week? *Dios mio.*"

"Well, we *do* have Holy Week. But not like this."

"But you have parades, of course?"

"No. No parades."

"No parades? *Caray.* Certainly you have parties and feasts?"

"No parties."

"*Ay de mi.* What do you do, then?"

"Mostly we just go to church and celebrate the birth of Jerry Fallwell."

She uncaps another longneck beer and places it before me. The bottle is not even cold. Cold beer isn't a thing here in Spain. She tells me this one is on the house. *Cortesía de la casa.*

"This America sound very strange, *señor.*"

"It is."

"But you are a religious man, no? This is why you are here, walking *el Camino?*"

I shake my head. "Not religious, no."

The room is mostly empty. There are a few old men sitting on stools, watching the TV. Ben Hur is winning his chariot race. A guy shuffles to the cigarette machine and buys a carton of Lucky Strikes. The parade is beginning outside. I can hear the drums beating. It sounds like a full-scale war is about to begin. Someone shoots a cannon that rattles all the glasses in the bar.

The barkeep's eyes are soft. She looks like she could be someone's grandmother.

"*Mijo.* I think you are very brave."

"Brave, no." I laugh. "I'm very foolish. Walking the Camino during Holy Week, without any plans."

"We have an old saying in Spain."

"Of course you do."

"Man plans, God laughs."

I place money on the counter and get off the stool. I hoist my backpack and fiddle. "Well, the joke's on me because I feel very stupid."

"*No estupido,*" she says in a gentle voice. "Not to me, and not to the *millones* of *ángeles* and saints who surround you right now."

I look around me. There are no saints. No angels. Only a tavern of people in simple clothes, watching *Ben Hur*.

"I don't see any *ángeles*," I say.

"Do not worry," she says with a wink. "They see you."

WE WALK INTO THE NEXT VILLAGE, COASTING on fumes. We are covered in splattered mud and sweat, clutching our backpacks, and on the perpetual lookout for a place to stay.

We knock on the hostel door.

The woman who opens the door utters four magic words.

"*Sí*, we have bed."

We are exhilarated, but we aren't sure whether we can trust this good news. Which is why I feel the need to clarify. I really don't want to get this wrong.

"A bed," I'm saying loudly, while also making the international hand-sign for *bed*. I press my palms together and rest my head against them and make a light snoring noise. "You have a *bed*? For tonight? A *bed*?"

She looks at me with an unmoving face. "What is wrong with this man?"

Then she storms off, leaving the door open.

"*Madre de Dios!*" she says. Then—I am one hundred percent sure about this—she cusses in Spanish.

We are left standing on the porch, unsure whether she

wants us to follow her or to perform an immoral act upon ourselves.

She stops walking and turns to face us.

"Are you going to just stand there with your faces hanging out or are you coming in?" Then she cusses again.

We show ourselves in.

We have a bed. Tonight. Us. A warm bed. With a shower! I could cry.

Even so, make no mistake about this, tonight's lodgings are nothing fancy. Tonight's hostel is small. And by "small," I mean the entire hostel is the size of a chiropractic exam room. Also, this place is—and I mean this in the nicest way possible—a total craphole. The bunkrooms have water spots on the walls, the ceiling is caving in, and the beds look like Club Med for lice. The tile floors are sticky from centuries of pilgrims' sweaty feet traipsing across them, smearing foot funk into the grout lines. I don't believe the staff has cleaned this place since the Spanish-American War.

But we don't care.

This place is heaven.

The first thing we do is use the showers. The bathrooms are in horrible shape. The shower stall smells like an infected belly button. As I am showering, the drain begins to overflow until water rises to my ankles. When I look into the growing lake surrounding me, there are tiny hairs in the water. The hairs are continually belching up from the drain like a kind of surrealist nightmare. Miniscule hairs, of all different colors and creeds, with the telltale pubic curl to them.

After we bathe, the innkeeper calls us in for supper. She is shouting our names and pronouncing them wrong.

"John and Jane!" she shouts to us. "You eat now!"

I look at the math teacher. "You heard the woman, Jane."

THE SUN IS SETTING AND THE WORLD IS PINK AND GRAY. John and Jane gather with the rest of the pilgrims for a grand communal dinner. There must be fifty or sixty pilgrims here tonight. Their jocular chatter fills the room. Many of them unbathed, in their stocking feet. People find their seats around the table. We are surrounded by hikers from many nations. Denmark, Taiwan, Bosnia, Sweden, Cape Town, Ireland, South Korea, France, Austria, Bolivia, Israel, Nigeria, China, Canada, Holland, and Jefferson County, Alabama.

I am so thirsty, it feels like my lips are cracking. The woman brings us clay pitchers, and everyone applauds her. We are all parched. But the pitchers do not contain water.

"No water today," she says.

For some reason, the innkeeper recommends not drinking tap water today. Evidently something is wrong with the water. I think she is telling me, in broken English, that the tap water has been contaminated from a shattered sewage line. Then again, she is speaking so fast, with such a heavy accent, that she might be saying there are glowing mushrooms growing in an attic in East Belgium.

Either way, the innkeeper is adamant about not drinking the water. She communicates this sentiment by pantomime: drinking from an imaginary glass, then clutching her throat with both hands and pretending to die. This country is marvelous.

She gestures to the clay pitchers, which all contain wine.

"You drink wine," she says.

We pilgrims are asking whether our host has bottles of water, saying we are willing to pay. Sorry, she replies, if you want bottles of water, go to a Holiday Inn. This is not a Holiday Inn, she is telling us. This is not the kind of place that offers beds *and* water. Quit acting so entitled and drink your wine, you tourist scum.

We all hang our heads. How presumptuous of us. We should be ashamed of ourselves, expecting drinkable water. So everyone drinks the wine liberally, even non-drinkers, because wine is all we have. The man next to me is from Wales and is a teetotaler. Even he is drinking the wine. We all drink from mismatched plastic tumblers and jelly jars.

The soup is simple, potatoes and leeks. It comes to the table in a soup pot that is big enough to cook an average-sized toddler. The bread is hard enough to sand oil stains from residential driveways. Still, we are all certain this is about to be the best food we've ever tasted. We are in Buckingham Palace tonight. That's how hungry we are.

The soup is passed around, family style. Everyone fills their bowls. But before we eat, someone taps their plastic tumbler with a fork. Regina, who is from Austria, stands and addresses the room. She suggests we all say grace by reciting the Lord's Prayer, taking turns, each in his or her own tongue. We all have so much to be thankful for, she is saying. We have beds. We have food. We know there are some pilgrims who do not have these things right now.

So all the pilgrims look around. This is going to take a while, we're thinking. There are so many of us. If we each take time to pray, the soup will be cold by the time the blessing is over. Still, Regina is right. Amazingly, nobody objects to her idea. Not even the atheists among us. Everyone is grateful tonight. Atheist and non-atheist alike.

So one at a time pilgrims stand and recite the Lord's Prayer to the rest of the table, speaking in their own language. The air becomes balmy with the feeling of gratitude. We have forgotten all about our food and are fully here together.

Each prayer spoken carries the unmistakable cadence of that familiar oration. The words are different, but the tone is the same. The Lord's Prayer has different personalities in each language. In French, the prayer is poetry. In German, it is declarative. In Korean, it is humble. In Russian, it is powerful. In Japanese, it is orderly. In Spanish, it is passionate. In Dutch, it is Dutch.

Then everyone looks to me.

It is my turn to pray.

"Where are you from?" Regina asks.

"Alabama," I say.

"Where is this Alabama?" asks a young woman from South Korea.

People around the table chuckle.

"Alabama is, uh . . . ," I am explaining. "Well, do you know where Tennessee is?"

The Korean woman wears a confused face. "I'm sorry, your accent is so difficult to understand. Tennessee?"

"Do you know where Atlanta is?" my wife interjects.

The Korean woman frowns.

"It's above Disney World," says the Frenchman beside me.

The Korean woman smiles. "Ah! Disney World!"

I fold my hands, close my eyes, and clear my throat. All heads are bowed. All hands are folded. I look at the bread and the wine, sitting on the table. But I cannot speak. My mouth is open. But no words are coming out.

IN FIRST-CENTURY ROME, CHRISTIANS WERE SLAUGHTERED by the hundreds of thousands. It was a federal offense to be a Christian. This was back during the days when Christianity was still a Jewish religion and had not blossomed into its Western form yet. Back then there were neither Trinities nor Apostle's Creeds nor Holy Bibles—the wealthy guys in pointy hats hadn't voted on which books should and shouldn't be in the Bible yet. No, in those days, sects of Christians, truthfully, didn't know what they believed, exactly. All they knew was that Teacher said, "Love the Lord your God . . . And love your neighbor as yourself."

Two million Christians were martyred, some scholars believe. They did not die for dogmas. If you would have asked an early Christian what his or her religion was, they would have answered, "Religion? I have no religion."

Whenever a Christian was arrested, he or she was thrown into a dungeon, foul and dark. They were treated like animals. They went to the bathroom on the floor; they slept with rats nipping at their ankles. Amazingly, they were scarcely alone in these prisons. Because every time a Christian was arrested, one of his or her brothers or sisters would show up, unannounced, volunteering to die alongside them. This visitor would usually arrive carrying fresh bread and a bladder of wine. The visitor was promptly arrested, of course. But that same evening, in their cell, if the guards allowed it, together they ate bread and wine before their death. They called this meal a "Love Feast."

Eventually, Rome had killed so many Christians that nobody was left to deliver the bread and wine. So Christian children started volunteering for the role of deliveryperson.

Tarcisius was one such boy. He was twelve years old. He volunteered to carry bread and wine to imprisoned Christians about to be executed. On his walk to the prison houses, he was attacked by a gang of thugs who suspected he was carrying food and wine. Tarcisius refused to give up the food. The thugs threatened to kill him if he didn't. Tarcisius told them to do what they must.

The twelve-year-old boy was beaten to death. They left him lying in the street. A few days later, a fellow Christian recovered Tarcisius's body, lying in a puddle of dried blood. The boy's corpse was clutching something against its chest. It was the bread and wine. Tarcisius never let them go. That's how important they were to him.

I am thinking about those martyrs now, as I look at the food on this table. The bread and wine. The heritage of my faith is coming to me. A faith based only upon one four-letter word.

My eyes grow hot with tears.

"Our Father . . . ," I begin.

I come from fundamentalist people. We were an aggressively religious people who made the Amish look fun-loving. We were hardshell evangelicals with no sense of humor. We did all the right things. Prayed all the right prayers. Gave ten percent. Our church dispatched missionaries to primitive nations to teach natives about a sovereign God who fiercely loved them and eagerly yearned for all people to repent and become American.

We did not watch R-rated movies, listen to secular radio, nor read magazines that did not feature Billy Graham or Oral Roberts on the cover. We were not allowed to use filthy language such as "gosh," "dang," "heck," and definitely not "for cripe's sake." Once, my cousin Ed Lee used the phrase "ignorant little butthole," whereupon he was dragged outside and shot.

We were teetotalers. We believed in full immersion. Our women wore skirts below the ankles and were prohibited from jeans, makeup, or perfume. Our fathers worked hard. Our mothers were frugal. My mother was so cheap she cut my hair herself, making swipes across my scalp with pre-World-War-II electric clippers until, finally, she pronounced that I would die a virgin.

In my childhood, Christianity was a tool of oppression. We talked about love, sure. But we had *much* more important things to worry about. Such as not winding up in an eternal place where demons commonly use pliers to pluck out your toenails.

We were told about a God who was always pissed off for some reason. This God was a riddle to me. I didn't understand his prevailing logic. Let's get this straight: God creates a race of humans, whom he loves very much, but somehow he is tangled up in a Vegas-style bet with the devil, wherein the devil wins all humans ever made unless God whacks his own kid. Are you with me so far? We humans legally belong to the devil, until God gets blood. So God works out a deal with the devil, and they agree on a pagan-style sacrifice. So Jesus volunteers to let God kill him. Problem solved, right?

Well, not exactly. This crucifixion, we are told in Sunday school, doesn't solve the *whole* problem. Meaning, the rest is up to you. You are still going to hell unless you say *precisely* the right words, in public, in front of all your friends and your aunt and everything, then you must get baptized, then you have to read your Bible every day, then you must believe exactly the right doctrines and do all the right things. And if, by chance, you were born with intellectual disabilities or—God forbid—born into the wrong culture where they don't believe this stuff: Sorry, Charlie. You're gonna burn.

I bring this up because I have prayed the Lord's Prayer a million and one times. Maybe more. But it's never had much of a meaning to me before. What exactly does *hallowed* mean? In my life, this prayer has always been uttered with drone-like tones, and the antique language has always been rendered benign.

But standing before these sweaty pilgrims, peering down at this great table, the Lord's Prayer feels like a very different thing.

". . . Which art in heaven, hallowed be thy name . . ."

Growing up, I desperately wanted to find my own spirituality. But I never could. You cannot find the depths of your own soul when religion is screaming at you. In fact, I can hear some of you already screaming at me now. Some of you reading this are so secure in your religious beliefs, whatever those might be. You hold all the answers; you know all mysteries of God; you've checked all the boxes; you've completed all the paperwork. There is little room left in your life for wonder. Many of you have likely already put this book down because I am an ignorant little butthole.

And, well, maybe I am.

Either way, religion is phony. At least the Americanized religion I come from is. Have you ever wondered why the number of American Christians is on a stark decline in our nation? America has twenty percent less Christians than it did twenty years ago. In the next few years, the trending numbers will keep going down. One day there won't be many left. Why is that? How can one of history's oldest faith traditions, a tradition people were *martyred for*, be declining? What does that say about this current brand of Christianity?

It says a lot.

Why do modern evangelical Christians cheerfully say, "Jesus loves you," while also detesting LGBTQ communities, Islamic people, Mormons, updated Cracker Barrel logos, SpongeBob SquarePants, Tide with Bleach, and certain breeds of cantaloupe? Why are these Christians so angry?

Also, how come there are 400,000 kids in the US foster-care system while over 235 million people identify as Bible-believing? Why are modern churches being housed in renovated Kmarts, naming themselves after non-transitive verbs such as "Elevate," "Alleviate," or "Constipate"? Why does your local Six-Flags-Over-Jesus church spend more of its budget on a golf-cart parking-lot ministry than on single moms who can't afford groceries? Why are there sixty-five very different Baptist denominations in the US? Sixty-five. And those are just the ones who are formally recognized. There are 238 separate Baptist member bodies throughout the world. Baptists can't even agree with *each other*, let alone with anyone else.

". . . Thy kingdom come," I say, "thy will be done, on earth as it is in heaven."

Tears are now falling down my cheek.

". . . Give us this day, our daily bread . . ."

A few pilgrims are rubbing my back. Others are weeping too. The room feels so warm, so unified. As I look at this food and wine, I am realizing that this simple meal, along with the clothes on my tired back and the love of strangers, represent all I currently own. And it is enough. It has always been enough. Love will always be enough. God is love, and evermore shall he be. The words of this prayer have never been so real to me before.

After my prayer, everyone says, "Amen."

A few people cross themselves.

Others are wiping eyes and blowing noses loudly into napkins.

The Korean girl beside me says, "What the hell did he just say?"

AFTER SUPPER, I BRING OUT MY FIDDLE. I AM FIDDLING IN the common area, sitting on the windowsill of an open window, overlooking an alleyway tangled with a network of clotheslines below. I'm playing "Let's Go Down to the Valley to Pray."

On the street beneath me are several Basque teenage girls who are just hanging out and playing some sort of game like hopscotch. They hear the fiddle and they start cheering for me. The girls then ask me to play something upbeat. So I play "Backstep Cindy." A square dance tune. The girls join arms and begin dancing. They are not bashful, the way American teens might be. These girls are free with their dance and free with their singing. They twirl and spin, moving in what appear to be traditional Basque steps. This whole scene strikes me as ancient and timeless. I am also thinking that something like this would never happen in America.

We do not dance in the street.

What would people think?

Soon, more townspeople join the dancing girls below. There are maybe ten people informally dancing now. On a nearby balcony from another hostel, I see other pilgrims who ask me to sing something. So I do. My singing voice is hoarse and tired, but the pilgrims are nice enough not to throw up.

Before long, there are several pilgrims gathering around me, drawn by the music. We are all singing, punctuated only by our laughter.

Then the mood becomes much more vulnerable between us as we share songs that are special to us and we explain why. One man sings a folk melody from Albania. Another woman offers a hymn from her homeland of Greece. A man from Ireland sings a lament. Then someone requests that the fiddler play "Amazing Grace."

I rosin my bow, then fine-tune the fiddle. The air kind of changes when I play this song. Everyone apparently knows the English lyrics to the familiar Anglican tune. Even the Basque girls on the street below are singing in perfect English. Soon, I hear distant voices across the street, also singing in English. It is Holy Week. And I am in a country that loves to sing. And we are singing the world's most popular folk song.

Younger pilgrims in the common area smoke cigarettes, gazing into the dusk, just listening. Others are clasping hands and singing harmony with eyes closed, as if they are praying. Those who are not singing are closing their eyes too. We've walked a long way to get here. It has to mean something.

A brilliant sun dips beneath the great Iberian Peninsula horizon. And just for a moment in time, during this Semana Santa, each person in this faraway village is my family. Each person belongs to me. And I belong to them. We are all related. Each heart, brother and sister, to one another. We are all loved. Young and old. Male and female. Rich and poor. Even a wretch like me.

My Daily Bread couldn't taste any better than it does today.

THE EIGHTY-THREE-YEAR-OLD WOMAN HAS BEEN opening her home to pilgrims since before I was born. Currently, she is bustling around her house, gathering fresh towels and soap for us. It's raining. We are standing in her doorway, drenched, cold, and looking about as content as wet Himalayan cats.

It's Easter Sunday. This is the biggest holiday in the entire country, but today feels more like the aftermath of Hurricane Andrew. There is a lot of flooding on roadways. In some places, the Camino has turned into a miniature river. Many of the local parades have been postponed. Which means that all the Spanish people are snugly inside their homes, preparing holiday food with their families, eating themselves into comas, taking multiple siestas, and watching *Spartacus*.

Meanwhile, we were walking in the driving rain.

"*Bienvenidos!*" says the old woman says to us.

The old lady speaks no English. But my six semesters of college *Español* courses are coming back to me. I am finally able to have Spanish conversations without too much stuttering.

Caring for pilgrims, I am learning from this woman, is a holy endeavor in Spain. Not just a hobby. Not just something you do on weekends. For some, acts of service are their life's work.

From what I glean, the woman's husband is dead. She has been aiding pilgrims ever since she was a young woman, because she feels this is her purpose in life. Her children are grown now, but they also help pilgrims. Her kids have grown up offering hospitality to *peregrinos*. They have never known a year of their lives when strangers weren't gallivanting through their homes, using the showers, helping themselves to the contents of their refrigerator. This is their life.

We shed our muddy boots at the woman's behest. The woman's son is soon on his knees, stuffing newspaper into our wet boots. His bare hands are deep inside our gross stink factories, and yet he is cheerful.

I tell him this is not necessary. He smiles and tells me it *is* necessary—the newspaper will help dry the boots, and dry boots will prevent blisters. He is unaffected by our nasty shoes and tells me to take off my socks next.

"My socks?"

"Si, *por favor.*"

"My socks are revolting," I say.

"Please, brother."

Humbly, I remove my wet socks. He takes them in his bare hands like they are ordinary, everyday objects. He is not repulsed. He is not squeamish. This man is dealing with our foulness without flinching.

"Thank you," he says.

Thank you.

He actually thanks me for handing him my disgusting socks.

This is not a mere profession for him but a *vocación*. A calling. I thank God for this calling. Because tonight all nearby hostels were full. Once again, there was no room at the proverbial inn. The proverbial Mary and Joseph, and their little proverbial Dutch baby, Christina, would've been compelled to keep hiking onward until they hit proverbial East-Bumble Timbuktu.

But the old lady took pity on us. She first spotted us as we trudged through the rain-soaked village, clutching our packs, wearing the same agonizing looks of those who have just left a prison camp.

"*Ven aquí!*" the woman said to us, motioning for us to come to inside.

So now we are warm. And we evidently hit the jackpot of all hostels too, because the woman tells us she has a brand-new endless water heater. Our showers can last as long as veterinary school if we like and she won't care, she explains.

Which is why I hug the woman.

We are barefoot, dripping in her hallway. We are filthy. And yet the elderly woman is not hesitant when I hug her. For this is Spain, she says. "We hug fifty times before breakfast in Spain."

Then she quickly releases me.

"*Apestas, mijo,*" she says, which can be translated as: "You stink, boy."

The shower is searingly hot. Almost obscenely wonderful. The math teacher and I wash our filthy clothes in the shower, using shampoo for detergent. Then we hang our clothes to dry on a windowsill. The upper level of the woman's house has been renovated into an apartment for pilgrims. Complete with full kitchen, bean bag chairs, sofas, a flatscreen, and an elliptical exercise machine. (God help the deranged pilgrim who requested an elliptical machine.)

The old woman sometimes feeds pilgrims, she says, but she has a family function for Easter tonight. So we are on our own for finding supper. Thus, Jamie and I leave for town, accompanied by Christina. We are all on the hunt for a market or a store or anywhere, really. Somewhere to buy food. The good news is, it's quit raining. The bad news is, there is but one mercado in town. The doors are locked, the lights are off, and the shades are drawn.

So we knock.

Nobody answers.

"This is not good," says Christina ominously.

Knock, knock, knock!

Still no answer.

"*Really* not good," I say.

Knock, knock!

Now it's raining again.

The math teacher invents a new cuss word.

Our stomachs are growling. We haven't eaten a proper meal since last night. This little market represents the deciding factor between feasting or fasting tonight.

Knock, knock!

But nobody is coming. Game over.

We all turn to leave with hangdog looks and gloomy faces. Back through the rain we shall walk. We shall go to bed hungry. Worse things have happened, of course. This is not the end of the world. But this definitely doth sucketh.

But then something happened.

It was almost like a Bible story.

And so it came to pass, in those days, that our three heroes were about to leaveth the market when a small, older Basque woman came to the mercado door to receiveth them. She, too, spaketh no English. *Ni una jota.* I inquired of the woman whether her store was open. She sighed, then shook her head at us the same way a mother shakes her head at a little boy who has been caught eating glue—not that I have ever done this.

"*Cerrado*," she says, shaking her head and pointing to an imaginary watch, which means "Closed."

"You come *mañana*," she says.

"*Comida*," I say, pleading. "*Por-fa*," I whine, giving her my best Little Orphan Annie face.

Her eyes roll. The woman begins to smile, but it's an annoyed grin. The kind of smile your mom gives you during church just before she swats your thigh with a hairbrush.

"*Prisa*," the woman says, clearly aggravated. "*Entra. Entra.*"

Oh, if there is a more beautiful word in this wonderful language than *entra*, I have yet to hear it. Granted, this woman is not in a great mood, and her market is the size of a residential walk-in closet, but she is telling us to *entra*. There is a God.

She calls us *mijo*. She tells us to hurry. Inside she has everything. Fresh cheeses, handmade breads, cured meats, fine chocolates, wine, pastries, beer. She prepares all the baked goods here herself, she says. A friend of hers makes the cheeses by hand from milk that comes from the sheep farmer next door. The wine is made just down the road; she points through the window at the winery.

She loads us down with food. Her kindness is punctuated with violent outbursts, reminding us in rapid Spanish just how foolish we are for having the audacity to bother her on this most sacred of holy days. We ought to be ashamed of ourselves. She wags her finger at us and I am worried she is going to grab a hairbrush.

We fill our packs with enough food to feed the People's Liberation Army. Christina and the math teacher are thanking her repeatedly in Spanish. I am offering to bear the woman's children. I do not get the impression this woman would appreciate a hug. So after our sales transaction I shake her hand. She smiles when I kiss her hand and thank her for her kindness.

"*Apestas, mijo,*" she says.

Which may be true. But someone up there is watching out for me just the same.

Happy Easter.

THIS IS THE FIRST TIME IN 1,300 YEARS A POPE HAS died during Easter festivities. A pope from a Latin country too. The death of Pope Francis is a huge deal. Huge. In America, news of the pope's death was still a big deal, don't get me wrong, and probably earned a slot on the evening news, with several internet headlines and newspaper stories. Maybe it was even mentioned on *Live with Kelly and Mark*. But in Spain, this news is bigger than 9/11.

We are walking on Easter Monday morning. The air is cool. We are alone, the math teacher and I. After hugs and tears, Christina has parted ways with us. She was meeting up with some people on the Camino and told us that she felt that the slowest member of our group was holding her back. Christina is very fit and would not specify *who* the slowest member of our group was, but she was staring in my general direction when she said these words.

At the precise moment Francis is pronounced dead, we are entering Nájera, a small village with a bell tower. The local villages come apart. In every market and café, the locals are in a kind of reverential shock when you speak to them. I don't think an earthquake could have caused more alarm.

"*El papa está muerto!*" they keep saying.

"The pope is dead."

The town is in full-mourning mode. Spanish women wear black shawls, weeping openly in the streets. There are groups of nuns and monks praying as they walk in formation, entering churches en masse. Bells are clanging across hillsides. People are shouting. This is such a big event, many of us non-Catholic pilgrims feel we should also honor it somehow. We are guests in this country. It only seems right.

So a few of us walk into La Iglesia de la Santa Cruz. I remove my hat. I take a pew alongside Diego, who is from Jalisco, and Taku, who is from Nagasaki.

It's silent inside this chapel, save for the sniffing of many noses.

Diego is praying in Spanish. Taku is taking pictures of the chapel.

This church altar is stunning. Made of more gold than I have ever seen. There are older women in the pew beside me, praying. They are weeping openly. "*Santa Maria*," they moan, their voices reverberating off the walls.

There is an old woman next to me. She rests a hand on mine. There are tears in her eyes.

"I'm sorry," I say to her.

It's a stupid thing to say, but it's programmed into my American brain.

"*Qué?*" she says.

"He was a great man," I say in Spanish.

She nods, then pats my hand lightly.

"*Santa Maria.*"

Soon it is time to walk again. We walk the Camino beneath a white-hot Spanish sun and the mood is somber. None of the pilgrims are speaking much on the trail. Nobody knows what to say. There are a lot of Catholics hiking with us today, and the pope is all they are thinking about.

"He was the voice of the poor," one Argentinian man says.

"He was a humble servant," says a woman from Mexico City.

"He fed the hungry," said an Italian man.

An Irish woman tells me it was the pope's words who first convinced her to walk the Camino a few years earlier. She says, "The pope once said that you can learn all things about God just by walking this road. Nothing else is needed. Just walk, and you will find God."

"The pope said that?" I asked.

She nods. "He did. Aye."

SIX OF US HAVE FALLEN IN TOGETHER, WALKING SIDE BY side for the last several miles. We are all strangers. All pilgrims. From different nations. There is dust clinging to our backpacks, mud covering our boots, and we all smell like something a diuretic horse produced. Each of us walks with a forward-leaning gait, a gait synonymous with pilgrims. We perpetually lean forward against the never-ending weight of the individual loads we carry. Some packs are heavier than others. As in life. And just like life, some move faster than their peers, while others move slower. But at this moment, for whatever reason, our individual paces have aligned. And now we are all together.

Six unlikely people, hiking a really long trail.

Out here, friends come and go. People's daily walks intersect, then diverge. Maybe your trails will converge again some-day. Maybe not. You might meet someone and form a con-nection, then never see this person again. You might meet someone who could piss off Mother Teresa; you will see this person every day.

We are covered in perspiration. The sound of our feet sounds like a band of rubber mallets beating earthen drums.

Richard, from Cork, sees the fiddle on my back. He speaks with an Irish brogue.

"What's your name?" he asks.

"Sean," I say.

He is impressed by this. "Sean, you say? Gaelic name. Do you spell it with the fada over the *A*?"

"Only on my birth certificate."

"Are you Irish?"

"Scotch."

"Well, nobody's perfect."

Richard is young, tall and lean, with an auburn mass of curly hair. He is holding the hand of his wife, Molly. They have walked for many miles, clasping hands, without letting go. Call it a hunch, but I'd guess they are newlyweds.

"Is that a fiddle on your back, Sean?"

"No flies on you."

"Will you be singing for us then, Sean?"

"Singing?" I reply.

"This is the Camino. We are supposed to sing."

Richard keeps pressing. So I finally give in. I sing in rhythm with my steps, gasping for oxygen. With my feeble voice, I am recounting the beloved Johnny Cash anthem of a male with the unfortunate title of "Sue." Everyone seems to know this song. Everyone applauds when I finish because this is more polite than gagging.

"Now it's your turn to sing," I say to Richard.

"Sing?" he replies. "You want me to sing, do you?"

"Aye."

So Richard sings in Gaelic. It is a haunting folk melody with consonants and vowels that almost sound like a language

I know. Maybe in my ancestral DNA, I have heard this language before. My Scot mother named me with a Gaelic name and I feel my blood rising as he sings.

We applaud.

Next, we turn to Molly. "Now it's your turn," we all say.

Molly is young and fair. Beautiful and brunette. She is originally from New Zealand and speaks like it. She is still holding Richard's hand. Heaven forbid she let go even for a moment. Molly sings a John Prine song, singing the lyrics with an Americanized countrified accent because, I can only assume, this is the only way she's ever heard the song done. Richard says she looks like an angel when she sings. Which is true. But the song she sings is a John Prine song about a young man who likes to sniff his girlfriend's panties.

After her racy song, we are not quite sure whether to applaud or pray for her.

"What is panties?" says Taku.

"Never mind," says Diego.

Next it is my wife's turn to sing. She sings Shania Twain's timeless opus to infidelity, "Whose Bed Have Your Boots Been Under?" You have to worry about this woman. She stops in the middle of the path to shake her pelvis. Suddenly Molly's song doesn't seem so shocking anymore.

Next it is Taku's turn to sing. Taku is small and lithe. He speaks almost solely Japanese, yet navigates this country alone, on a budget of mere pennies. We have become close with Taku. Over the past day, we have walked with him more than anyone else. It is amazing how much English and Spanish he has learned in only a few weeks on the Camino. He is the happiest young man I have ever met. He laughs often. He is meek, soft-spoken, and sincerity is painted all over his words.

"Sing for us, Taku," I say, patting his slender shoulder.

"Sing?" he says.

"Yes!" we are all shouting, "Sing, sing!"

"I no sing."

"Please, Taku!"

"No sing."

"You gotta sing!"

"Me no sing."

"Taku!"

He is silent for a beat.

We all stop walking while he gathers his thoughts.

Then Taku says, "I sing children song. Song about spring in Japan."

His voice is shaky, and he is trembling from nerves because we are all watching him. He closes his eyes when he sings. The melody is simple. But he sings honestly and without restraint. A few of us are wiping tears when he tells us in shattered English how spring reminds him of his mom, and how he misses his mom so badly because she lives so far away from him now that he is an adult.

Next, we turn to Diego. Diego operates a *taqueria* in Jalisco. He is a foody, with long hair, earrings, and his blood pressure is low enough to concern a cardiologist. We have had many long conversations about life and the meaning of existence, and about the destructive lower-intestinal effects of various tacos. He has shared with me his dreams and aspirations. He wants to be a professional chef someday.

He sings "Cielito Lindo," which is a song we all know the chorus to.

"*Ay ay ay ay!*"

Applause.

We walk onward. The sun is getting hotter. The Spanish countryside is brilliant golden fields of rapeseed blanketing the countryside. Yellow for as far as the naked eye can see.

"Maybe we should all sing something together," suggests Molly. "Something everyone knows?" says Diego.

"Good idea," says another.

"How about some Skynyrd?" says my wife.

"Maybe a hymn?" adds someone else.

We are quiet for a bit. The rhythm of our shoes crunching on gravel.

"We could sing 'Amazing Grace,'" Diego says.

Taku speaks in broken English. "I do not know the words to this song."

"It's okay," Diego replies, glancing at the midday sun. "We don't need the words. We're experiencing them right now."

ODAY HAS BEEN THE MOST DIFFICULT HIKE SO FAR because the weather has been uniquely hot. Many pilgrims on the trail have been helpfully telling us the current temperature, but most of these pilgrims are from countries that use the metric system and so the temperature is always thirty-eight liters, or ten kilograms, or 1,200 millimeters, or three degrees centipede.

We enter the town of Grañón in the afternoon. We collapse on the church steps and guzzle the last of our water.

The stone streets are empty for siesta. The entire Spanish world has shut down to observe their daily food stupor. Good luck finding an open *tienda*. Let alone a place to sleep. We are told by experienced Camino hikers that there are forty percent more pilgrims walking the Camino than there are albergue beds on this trail. I can attest to this being true inasmuch as we have not been able to easily find a bed since our feet touched Spain.

You never get used to this lodging search. Every morning feels laced with uncertainty.

This morning, after striking out at several different hostels and albergues, we decided to try an albergue in an old church that we'd heard about. Apparently, no matter how full they are, the *hospitaleros* do not turn pilgrims away.

Jamie and I recline on the church steps, heads resting against stone walls, covered with dirt, wearing grimy boots, with U-Hauls strapped to our backs, hoping against hope that the *hospitaleros* will have mercy on us.

The village of Granón looks like something from a low-budget spaghetti Western production. The town is dusty, ancient, and made entirely of stone and terracotta. The center-piece of the hamlet is the sixteenth century church of San Juan Bautista. The rock structure stands like a prehistoric behemoth in the middle of the archaic village. The cobbled street leading to the church is paved with stones worn smooth from centuries of pilgrim feet.

Granón dates back to 885, when King Leon Alfonso III ordered a castle to be built on a hill during the Reconquista. The locals, *Granóneros* or *Granóneras*, are rural people who mostly work in cattle or farming.

In the church courtyard nearby, we see pilgrims relaxing. Many are freshly showered. Their hair is wet. Their feet are clean and bare. They are wearing lounge clothes, lightly drying their heads with towels. And I am already having deep, almost illicit fantasies about hot showers.

I get up and start looking for a *hospitalero*. I meet a nun who does not speak English.

"You have beds?" I ask her.

She smiles, then shrugs and walks away.

So I find a volunteer, a heavyset man with olive skin, wearing a windbreaker.

"You have beds?" I say.

"*Sí*, beds. Yes."

"How much?" I ask, making the international sign for money.

The volunteer just looks at my finger and thumb rubbing together.

"How much *money*?" he says.

"*Sí*," I say. "*Precio*?"

"No price. Is free."

"Free?"

The volunteer smiles bigly. "*Sí*. Can you wash dishes?"

WE REMOVE OUR BOOTS AND PLACE THEM INTO A STONE chamber. We are led up a narrow, winding staircase in our stocking feet. The staircase is dark and musty, made from rough-hewn rocks with a strong *Count of Monte Cristo* meets *Silence of the Lambs* vibe. We are taken to a room with a plank-wooden floor covered in blue high school wrestling mats.

"What are these mats?" we ask.

The volunteer smiles. "Your beds."

We are informed that this is not an albergue, in the traditional sense of the word. This is a tenth century *hospital*, in the Spanish sense. *Hospital*, meaning you will probably die here. Grañón has been serving pilgrims this way for the last one thousand years. Hundreds of thousands, maybe even millions, of pilgrims have slept on this very floor. The volunteers who run this place maintain the old ways. Nothing has changed in a thousand years. We are living the way pilgrims would have lived ten centuries ago if they'd had wrestling mats. The *hospitalero* also informs us that, in addition to sleeping on the wooden floor, just as in the tenth century, we will also be cooking everyone's dinner tonight.

"Cooking?" we say.

"*Sí.*"

It is a communal supper. All the pilgrims are expected to pitch in and prepare the food. But before we begin cooking, however, we're told that all the pilgrims must first vote and elect a head chef. For this position, the volunteer says, we'll need a pilgrim with organizational skills, who is good with numbers and possesses the unique ability to lead with the finesse of a totalitarian government.

Everyone votes for my wife.

Within minutes, the math teacher and I are in the kitchen preparing dinner for a group of thirty-odd pilgrims. We are tired, unshowered, in our stocking feet. But there is a cheerful atmosphere in the kitchen, which might be due to all the wine that is flowing. There is so much wine being poured among pilgrims tonight that sometimes I can't remember my wife's name.

The ambience is convivial. People are laughing and making jokes and just generally having a great time. Those of us in the kitchen are even happier than the general population of pilgrims because we are the ones pouring the wine.

I am chopping onions, preparing pasta, while Jamie cooks the beef and Daithi, a software engineer from Ireland, preps baked potatoes while simultaneously teaching me to cuss in Irish. The kitchen is about the size of a water heater closet, only with less headroom. We learn that this kitchen has no working oven, so we must use the local bakery's oven to cook the potatoes. The bakery is located down the street, and we are told we must carry a dozen trays of potatoes across town. This is a cherished tradition at Grañón, marching through the town square with baking sheets full of potatoes, singing gaily, careful not to drop the potatoes and ruin everyone's supper. Or worse, spill our wine.

So a few of us pilgrims promenade through the village carrying baking sheets full of sliced, uncooked potatoes, singing "Ninety-Nine Bottles of Beer on the Wall" since we cannot find another song that we all know the words to except "The Wheels on the Bus Go Round and Round."

Townspeople pass us and do not bat an eyelash.

Mid-song, I trip over a cobblestone and fall flat on my backside, but somehow managed not to drop the potatoes. I am pretty sure I have broken my tailbone or given myself a subdural hematoma. But Daithi, who apparently has some medical training, examines me carefully and prescribes more wine.

Soon I am good to go.

We rush back to the church as our potatoes, across town, are now cooking in the bakery oven, and we finish preparing the rest of our supper in the hostel kitchen, which seems to have shrunk since we left. About thirty minutes later, a local messenger from the bakery enters the kitchen. He is out of breath when he arrives. He tells us the potatoes are finished cooking. We offer him wine and ask him what the hell potatoes he's talking about.

"The *papas*," he explains.

"Oh, yes! The *papas!*" we say, because somewhere, far in the recesses of our brains, we can recall that at some point, this supper vaguely involved potatoes. Also, my tailbone is killing me, but I can't figure out why.

"Come!" the messenger says. "The *papas* are ready!"

We are also told that all pilgrims and *hospitaleros* at the albergue must march down the street together to retrieve the cooked potatoes; this is an ancient San Juan church tradition dating back to olden times, which pilgrims reverently call, "Getting the potatoes." The ancient tradition also stipulates that all pilgrims who accompany us to get the potatoes must sing as we march and make a loud noise. We are to demand our potatoes from the baker, who is supposed to refuse to give us our potatoes unless we sing more songs. Also—I can't believe I left this part out—we members of the kitchen crew are expected to wear tutus and wigs.

"We're supposed to wear what?" I say.

Daithi holds a pink and yellow tutu up to the light. "We're going to need more wine."

And so it came to pass, that on April 22, the Year of Our Lord, that my wife and I, wearing full tutu regalia, with colorful wigs on our heads, led a parade of thirty pilgrims through the antiquarian streets of Grañón, carrying trays of cooked potatoes in our hands, while singing "Play That Funky Music White Boy."

SUPPER IS OVER. EVERYONE IS STUFFED. BUT THE NIGHT'S festivities are not over. The *hospitaleros* have now grown solemn, and all the laughter in the dining hall dies as they tell us there is one more thing to do before we are allowed to sleep. Soon, the *hospitaleros* gather all pilgrims into the cathedral's dark choir loft, which is cool and damp, lit only by flickering candles.

The chapel is tall and spacious. The stonework surrounding you is cold to the touch. The massive golden altar, the *Retablo Mayor*, was crafted in the 1550s and depicts the life of John the Baptist. It's amazing to think that the most exquisite art in the world was not placed in a big museum or a great metropolitan city, but in a tiny, dusty village. The art stands here simply to remind all pilgrims that our humble souls are somehow worthy of all the beauty God has to offer.

One of the volunteers flips on a light, which illuminates the altarpiece, gilded in Spanish gold. The vision is arresting. Whereupon one of the *hospitaleros* named Jose plays a splintered guitar. Jose asks me to join him on my fiddle. I have carried this fiddle on my back for the last a hundred and forty miles. I have been playing it more than I ever thought I would, at every camp, every café, and every albergue. But I have never played in a church.

Jose asks me to sing a hymn, if I know one. Any hymn will do. So I play "Lean on Me." A few pilgrims sing along. Then Jose plays a John Lennon song, which is weird in a Catholic church. But when in Rome. Next, it's my turn to sing something. So I sing "It Is Well with My Soul." My tired voice reverberates across ancient walls as though it is not my voice at all. The fiddle music slaps against the walls, bouncing off stones, and it sounds like I am playing ten fiddles at once.

The *hospitaleros* tell us this seems like a good time to share our reasons for walking the Camino. We are allowed to say whatever we want, whether it is a prayer, a poem, or a story about ourselves. They pass around a large candle and everyone takes turns speaking. I count fourteen different languages being spoken tonight. We have no idea what most of our fellow pilgrims are saying, but you can tell when they pray. And their prayers sound important because most of them are blowing their nose between sentences.

Crying, we discover, is a lot like yawning. A French woman across from me is weeping. A silver-haired man, a bricklayer from Wales, begins sobbing; today is his sixtieth birthday. He tells us all he has ever wanted to do, since childhood, is find God, but his religion was so strict, he felt that God was out of reach. He's learning on this Camino that God has been with him all the time. And he's learning that he's actually been walking the "Camino" since he was born. We all walk the Camino, he says. Every day, we walk.

A young man from Norway tells the group he had cancer and he is in remission. He says for most of his treatment, he thought God hated him. But now he knows better; he knows that his cancer was a gift. That suffering is a gift. Someday we will all understand that suffering is holy business, he says. To suffer is to know God.

A college-age girl from Ghana speaks openly about her mother's suicide, and how she has felt alone all her life. Like nobody sees her. Like nobody cares about her. But here on the Camino, she realizes that people love her, and have loved her all along, and that it was *she* who developed a hard shell to keep people away. Because she did not want to be loved. Because being loved is being vulnerable. And being vulnerable means that she can be hurt again. But now she wants to be loved. She wants love more than water. More than food. More than life itself. She just wants someone to hold her. So many of us take turns hugging her. When I hold her, I'm not sure whether I am the one holding her or whether she is holding me, because all my life I have wanted these same things.

A few of the pilgrims keep their words short. You can tell they aren't sure what to think about all this mushy, lovey-dovey stuff. They are guarded; maybe even a little hostile, it seems. A few leave the circle and go to bed. Nobody remarks about it. But overall, everyone is feeling the love in the room, even if a few are cautious.

The candle is finally passed to me.

I am speechless for a few moments.

The young woman's words about suicide have touched me so profoundly, I can hardly speak. Suicide changed my life too. I was eleven years old when I became a man. My uncle took me out into the woods and said that I would no longer be a little boy. He said I had to be the man of my family. Especially with my mother going catatonic. He said it was up to me to make sure the laundry got washed and that my little sister got meals. And if I had to get a job, well then, dammit, get a job. Take care of your family however you can. It's your responsibility, boy. He said he would do his best to help out, but he already had a family of his own, and this is what men just do. And yes, it sucks, and yes, it's a raw deal, and no, it's not fair, but this is the hand God dealt you, so suck it up.

My new role would separate me from those my age. I would age forty years overnight. I would become a freak. I would be blackballed by boys my age. Children do not understand trauma and abuse. They understand it even less when it happens to someone they know. I disappeared from my friends' lives. Kids quit calling me. I stopped going to school.

I have never belonged. And I have never felt loved. Not entirely. All I want sometimes is to be held like a baby. I want a mom I never had. I want to tuck myself into the folds of some Eternal Mother's skirt and be held. I want her to love me so deeply, so maternally, that I get lost in her arms. But suicide robs that privilege from your life. Suicide robs everything, you think to yourself. Years later, however, you come to realize that suicide robbed nothing of you. You were the one robbing yourself.

And as I hold the candle, I'm thinking about all this. I'm also trying to think of what to say to this room of people. What are my words going to be? Who will be my mother? Who will be my father? Who is going to hold me? Who is going to love me? Am I enough?

All that comes to my mind is a poem I learned in grade school. We learned it for Saint Patrick's Day. We sang it as a song, but the poem itself is older than the walls of this church. And I'm starting to think the pilgrim was right, the one who said suffering pushes you closer to the One whom you have known all your life. The One who has loved you before you were even born has always been with you.

I see it so clearly, holding this candle. The religious fanatics were wrong. There are no special prayers to pray. There are no rule books to follow. The One Who Loves You has been here all along, an intimate part of your everyday life. He is father and mother. He is brother and sister. He is lover and friend. He is the molecular reaction within your body. Every miracle of nature. Every blink of your eye, every breath you take. This Divine Love would no more leave you alone than you would leave your own baby unattended in a shopping mall.

I recite the poem through tears:

Christ with me,
Christ before me,
Christ behind me,
Christ in me,
Christ beneath me,
Christ above me,
Christ on my right,
Christ on my left.
Christ when I lie down,
Christ when I sit down,
Christ in the heart of every man who thinks of me,
Christ in the mouth of every man who speaks of me,
Christ in the eye that sees me,
Christ in the ear that hears me.

Then we all slept on our wrestling mats.

UEN CAMINO," SAYS ED, WHO IS STANDING ON the sidewalk outside the market in Villamayor. "Buen Camino," I reply.

This sets off a chain reaction of "Buen Caminos" among pilgrims. You are always saying these words. Every few moments, you are speaking them to a fellow pilgrim. Soon they become second nature. You don't even think about them anymore.

We are all standing outside the small market. There are about twenty-five, maybe thirty of us hapless, fatigued pilgrims here. We are sticky with perspiration, covered in grit, each of us wearing the same clothes we wore when starting this trail many weeks ago. Same pants. Same shirt. Same boots. Same outfits, washed in the same communal showers and sinks, each evening, over and again, then hung to dry on the same hostel balconies, spreading our deadly armpit fumes across the breadth of Spain.

We form a haphazard line outside Villamayor's one and only market as we wait for the shop owner to arrive so we can all buy our individual suppers.

Another few pilgrims arrive.

"Buen Camino."

"Buen Camino."

"Buen Camino."

The pilgrims are getting fussy. Pilgrims always get fussy when they are hungry. We are on the cusp of grumbling because the market sign says this store opens at 5:00 p.m., and yet it is already 5:32 and no employees are in sight. Shop signs mean nothing in Spain, we have learned. A shop can advertise that it opens at 9 a.m. and closes at 10 p.m. and yet remain closed for three or four papal administrations. This is Spain. There are no "set hours" for anything.

The store windows are dark. The town seems empty. Siesta is underway. We are all a little concerned. Because no market equals no supper. No supper equals crappy sleep. No sleep equals a difficult walk tomorrow. And we have three hundred and fifty miles left to walk.

More pilgrims arrive. The "Bueno Camino" butterfly effect lasts for about five minutes.

Then.

A car.

"Car!" someone shouts.

Everyone's conversations stop.

Pilgrims all hold their collective breath as the car swings into a nearby parking place. It is a minicar, the kind common to Europe, about the size of a roller skate. The car parks, then just sits and idles for a bit.

We are staring at the car like we can unlock the doors using only our eyeballs. But nobody is exiting the vehicle. The car just idles.

"Do you think it's the shop owner?" one pilgrim says.

"I hope so," someone says.

"Everyone just be patient," says another pilgrim.

"I'm from Jersey," adds another. "We don't do patience."

The car shuts off.

"They're turning off their car!"

A woman and her son leisurely crawl from the vehicle. The woman carries jangling keys in hand. She smiles at us when she sees us all standing in the street akin to shoppers on Black Friday

FRUTAS

looking for Beanie Babies. You can tell she is a proud woman. She walks with a swagger. She does not look thrilled to be here. Very few Spanish shopkeepers, I have discovered, are ever happy to have much business.

"Uh-oh," says one pilgrim. "She's gonna tell us she's closed."

"Just be cool."

"I am not leaving this sidewalk without food," says another.

The shop owner stands on the sidewalk, staring us down. She is scowling. She looks like she is about to break some very bad news.

Then a smile plays at the corners of her mouth as she says with a thick Spanish accent, "We are open."

Cheering ensues.

All pilgrims break into applause. I have never applauded the opening of a grocery store, but there is a first time for everything. Someone even throws their hat into the air. Others are hugging each other and jumping like we have all just witnessed a Red Sox victory. Spanish locals in nearby balconies, fully rested from their four-hour siestas, even put down their brandy snifters long enough to applaud along with us.

Then, madness.

Thirty-odd hungry pilgrims charge into a tiny mercado. Soon, there are dozens of pilgrims crowding each aisle, all wearing looks of rapture on their faces. We are famished, and this is a place with seemingly limitless food. We are already clearing the shelves, and the shop owner hasn't even turned on the lights yet. We are giddy over the smallest pleasantries this store has to offer.

"They have mayonnaise!" one pilgrim shouts.

"Pickles!" shouts another.

I see Hūn, a marine in the South Korean military. I am told South Korean marines are the best of the best, the toughest of the tough. Hūn is carrying a Coca-Cola and shouting, "Coke! They have Coke!" Hūn says this in the same tone of voice one might use to shout, "It's a boy!"

I see Stafanie, from the Netherlands. Stefanie has already lost weight on this trail and is nearly unrecognizable. Her skin looks like it is glowing. She says, "They have green beans!"

The hottest item in this store is definitely the fresh veggies—which are limited. Everyone wants salad because we've all been forced to eat packaged food for so long that we have forgotten what organic matter tastes like.

One pilgrim, Tadgh, from Ireland, buys a head of iceberg lettuce, which turns out to be the last head of lettuce in the whole store. The bruised and wilted lettuce looks like it's been sitting in the cooler since Reagan was in office. But, hey, it's lettuce.

Everyone sort of gathers around Tadgh with beautiful excitement, gazing at his leafy green treasure.

"You found lettuce," someone says in awe.

"Wow, you're so lucky," another says.

Tadgh smiles at the hyenas surrounding him. "Would you like some?" he says.

And although this young man has no obligation to do so, he chooses to split his head of lettuce among the pilgrims on the sidewalk, using his pocketknife. He shares lettuce with any pilgrim who wants some. In the end, Tadgh has no lettuce remaining for himself.

"That's okay," Tadgh tells me with a big smile. "I can have

lettuce some other time."

Meantime, I am buying cold beer. At the beer fridge, I run into Shū yi, a young woman from Taiwan who is walking the Camino by herself. Shū yi is maybe three feet tall and in her twenties. Her mother died last year, and Shū yi's mom always wanted to walk the Camino. She is doing this for her mom. She looks like a grade schooler.

"I am going to drink so much beer tonight!" she exclaims.

Shū yi and I become fast friends.

We open two cans of beer, right there in the store, and toast.

"What should we toast to?" she asks.

"To groceries," I say.

We touch the tips of our cans together.

Shū yi says, "Maybe we can toast to moms too."

Her face is smiling, but her brown eyes aren't.

"Sure," I say. "Let's toast to moms."

We toast again, then we hug each other and laugh. And I'm trying to think of another instance in my life when I would embrace a complete stranger and make toasts in the middle of a supermarket.

"Isn't this great?" Shū yi says.

"Isn't what great?"

She gestures to all the people in the rundown market. "This."

People are charging through the aisles with armfuls of items, smiling from temple to temple.

"All us pilgrims," she says, "being so happy over the smallest things. It is not this way in Korea."

"It's not this way in the US either."

"I feel like we are part of a big family."

"It is pretty great."

Shū yi purchases enough beer to supply a small country, then with a farewell wave, she says to all in the store, "Buen Camino!"

"BUEN CAMINO, SHŪ YI!" shouts every pilgrim in earshot.

Here's to moms.

Libro Dos

After we showered, we went down to the bar, grabbed a beer, and sat out on the patio. We noticed different tables where middle-aged people were sitting with older adults in wheelchairs. Of course, chatty Sean struck up a **conversation and** we learned about a nursing home nearby. People regularly check their parents out and bring them to this bar.

The man and his father were both having a beer. The woman and her mom were playing some sort of game.

It moved me to see adult children spending the afternoon with their elderly parents. Memories flooded my mind, of afternoons spent with my mother— often not saying much, just enjoying a breeze and having a cocktail together. I miss her, but know that she is with me every step I take on this journey.

OU WERE MADE TO WALK. IT REALLY IS THAT SIMple. I wish I'd learned this sooner.

Namely, because in my life, I've never actually known what I was made for. As a boy I thought I was designed to be a starting pitcher. When I was a teenager, I believed fervently God had called me to be a photographer for the *Sports Illustrated*'s swimsuit issue. As I aged, life became more complicated. I started to believe, like many Americans, that I was created solely for the purpose of finding a fulfilling career. When I got a little older, I realized this wasn't true. I realized I was uniquely and wonderfully designed to go forth and find adequate health insurance.

But it's not true. None of this is true. Your designation on earth is much simpler. Much more basic. You were given two feet. You were given two intricately, sophisticatedly engineered, complexly muscled legs, and a highly synchronous nervous system. And you were given these things for a much higher purpose than seeking out strong Wi-Fi.

You were made to move.

Walking is one of your grandest purposes on this earth. Now, before you write me off as a complete nutcake, imagine this: You are the richest person in the world. You have all the success anyone could ever dream of, all the wonderful things you want, all the love you can stand. Now imagine that you cannot move. You cannot walk. You are completely inert. Stuck in a bed. All you can do is blink your eyes.

Walking is a holy endeavor. Movement is spiritual. Shuffling one's feet has some sort of higher purpose to it. There is no way to explain this until you feel it. You once knew this, of course. But you forgot this along the way.

While walking, your brain grows quieter. And you begin to sense another part of yourself, lying beneath it all. Beneath the noise. A part of your body you hardly ever "feel" anymore. When you walk you sense your own soul. Sure, you've always known your soul is there. But being aware of your own soul is a lot like "being aware" of your own spleen. Most times, you cannot feel it.

But make no mistake, your soul is definitely there. Deep beneath your blood vessels, somewhere under your breath. Often, your brain is merely speaking too loud to hear the soul's poetry. For the soul's tiny voice is often overpowered by logic, reason, and your profound need for rationality.

But as you walk, you can hear your soul speaking. As you ascend hillsides, traversing mountainous vineyards, passing two-thousand-year-old villages, your soul says strange things to you. Things you wouldn't really expect. Things like:

Nice to finally be talking with you again.

Remember when you were a kid and we used to be so close?

Why are you so sad?

Wait, you're immediately thinking to yourself. Is this *my* soul speaking? Why is it talking to me like it's not part of me? Good question.

So maybe it's not the soul at all that you're talking to. Maybe the soul is simply an internal telephone. Perhaps you're really having a conversation with the Operator. Maybe the Operator has always been with you, present in your very soul, always talking to you. Moreover, maybe the Divine is talking with every human being the same way it talks to you. Maybe all the dogmatic persons who so often claim that God *only* speaks to official club members are profoundly and exquisitely full of livestock excrement.

God talks to everyone.

After bouts of long, soulful silence on the Camino, soon it's time to talk. You find that you must talk. Talking is as important as walking. Sometimes you will talk like it is your full-time job. Sometimes you will talk even more than you walk. Everyone talks eventually. Even the most silent on the trail. The soul must talk. It must purge itself. It must get it all out.

As a result, you as a pilgrim will hear a lot of talking on the Camino. You hear the innermost thoughts of your fellow pilgrims. You hear their souls speaking to you:

"My mom is terminally sick right now," says the thirty-year-old Mexican woman. "All my mom has ever done in her life is work. Her life has had so very little joy. Work, work, work. I am walking to Santiago for the miracle of her healing. But also to celebrate the beauty of her motherhood."

The twenty-three-year-old Italian boy: "I recently renounced my infant baptism in the Catholic Church. I did this in front of my mother and father and all the people because I do not like hypocrisy. I stood and formally declared that I am no longer Catholic, I am an atheist. My mother cried so hard. I think you call it being 'debaptized' in English. I am done with God."

And yet he is walking the Camino. For the third time.

A nineteen-year-old South Korean girl: "I want to see the whole world before I marry and do all the cooking and cleaning and make babies and get fat."

The sixty-four-year-old man from Poland: "I walk the Camino because my wife always wanted to do it, and now she is gone and she will never have that chance. Brain cancer took her when she was only sixty years old."

The young woman from Lincoln, Nebraska: "I was abused as a little girl. I need healing. I want to trust people again. But I don't. I sleep in the hostels with a knife under my pillow. I pray that nobody will ever hurt me again."

The thirty-three-year-old guy from Japan: "In Japan we are

so strict and we work too hard. My parents are honorable people, but they work so much that they are missing their own lives."

The twenty-nine-year-old flight attendant from England: "I just got out of a bad relationship, and I need to believe that the real me is still someplace deep down inside. Somewhere. I suppressed her for so long, I'm not sure she's inside me anymore. Pray that I can find my voice again."

The older woman from the Netherlands: "I search and search for a way to find joy, but I have never found it in my life. But out here, it turns out, joy was inside me all along. All I had to do was be courageous enough to find it."

The fifty-two-year-old Italian: "My father owned a small vineyard, and he made the best wine. He was a happy man and my best friend. When he died, I tried to take over his vineyard, but I cannot do it. So we were forced to sell vineyard. I cry so hard. No wine will ever taste like his. No man will ever be like him. I walk for his memory."

The forty-nine-year-old woman from Oregon: "I came here to escape politics. But the first week all I kept hearing about was politics. I was so mad. All anyone did out here was talk politics. I almost went home because I was so pissed. A few days later, I finally discovered why everyone was talking about politics. Because *I kept bringing it up*."

The sixty-three-year-old Hungarian man: "I never realized how arrogant and pigheaded I was until my divorce. I learned how angry and vengeful I can be. I believe that God can change me if I let him. He is using Plantar fasciitis to change me."

Frank, an older Australian man from Melbourne: "Last night our albergue had no hot water and all the pilgrims were so angry. But not me. For some reason I was not bothered at all. That's the Camino. Things that would normally aggravate you in real life don't bother you here. When I get home, New Frank isn't going to get bent out of shape about little things. That's not who I am anymore. I am New Frank. Say hello to New Frank."

The sixty-nine-year-old former priest from Italy: "I once

had a nervous breakdown. I got defrocked from my position of leadership. I lost everything. I was going to end my own life by hanging myself. But then I come out here, and I find the answer to life. I see it all so clearly. And I am ashamed that I ever considered ending my life for such foolish reasons.

"A lot of people are out here because they think they are searching for God. But the Camino cannot help you find God, for God is not missing. God is everywhere. And you already know him very well. He has always known you. He has no name. It matters not what other cultures call him. It matters not how our pitiful man-made religions have gotten him all wrong. What matters is you already know him. God is life. God is love. God is the interconnectedness of all things. God is every breath you take. God is the nutrients in your blood, the minerals in your bones, the electrical impulses that make your heart beat, your highest thought, your strongest joy. He is your vision. He is your hearing.

"You know him even if you don't believe in him at all. You know him because he is making you alive right now. He is not bound by your tiny brain's belief system of rules, sacraments, officiation, and religious rites. God is yours. Just like your heart is yours. Just like your kidneys are yours. In the same way, you are his. Your soul already knows what I am saying is true. Just ask it."

Amazing what you can learn by walking.

WE ARRIVE IN BURGOS AFTER A LONG, *LONG* walk through the unforgiving and detrimental sun. We are sunburned, thirsty, sore, fatigued, and our skin is covered in a fine layer of crystalized salt from evaporated sweat.

Today's weather is hot. Unmercifully hot. This might be the hottest day we've experienced yet. The heat makes the miles go by slower. Sometimes the days go by so sluggardly it is as though we have only hiked a few feet since breakfast. I'm dazed from dehydration. A little delirious. I'm not sure where I am anymore. Our lives revolve around the Camino now. The Camino is all we know. All we've ever known. All there is to know. I feel like we've been walking the Camino since we were toddlers.

Burgos is big and energetic and a great place to restock supplies. This is why most pilgrims have chosen to stay the night here. Plus, it's just too hot to keep walking today. We decide to stay in Burgos too. What I wouldn't give for a beer cold enough to break your teeth and a wedge of cheesecake roughly the size of the unabridged edition of *Gone with the Wind.*

When we enter Burgos, the temperature seems even hotter. Burgos is a metropolitan city. There is pavement everywhere. Pavement holds heat. You can feel the hotness radiating through your soles, until your shoes become soft and melty, akin to walking across a waffle iron.

Burgos is busy today. There are people everywhere. The International Writer's Union, Local No. 12, requires me to describe Burgos as "teeming with life." We are not prepared for such a sprawling cosmopolitan world. We have been hiking through wilderness, across mountains, through forests. Burgos is a shock to the system. The pedestrians here all wear designer clothes, designer shoes, and designer sunglasses that cost more than my truck. Even school children we pass on the street, lingering in doorways, are better dressed than your average American congressperson.

This is an uppity place, you can tell. Namely, because a few pedestrians on the sidewalk—this has happened more than once—actually plug their noses and sneer when I pass by. This happens four or five times. The first time it happened, it was a large group of young women who looked like they stepped out of an issue of *Vogue*. They covered their noses as they passed me on the sidewalk. Next, a young family all plugged their noses as they walked by, and the little boy stuck his tongue out at me.

"Do I smell *that* bad?" I ask my wife.

But my wife could not hear me asking because she was walking five hundred feet ahead of me to avoid being downwind.

So, the Burgos vibe is definitely not the friendly, "Anthony Quinn" vibe we have been experiencing throughout the rest of Spain thus far. Burgos feels more like New York City's Upper West Side during a funeral procession for the former CEO of Louis Vuitton. In short, I feel unwelcome here.

And it's not just a feeling. We *are* unwelcome here. The cashiers in shops and cafés do not smile at us. Many shop employees will hardly speak to us, even though I am speaking my best construction-jobsite Spanish. One woman working behind the counter at a local bakery actually ignores me until I finally leave. No matter how many times I ask her a question, she pretends I don't exist and simply helps another customer instead.

I am starting to get downhearted. I am already worn out and sunbeaten. But now I'm being discriminated against. This is not bringing up good feelings within me.

To get out of the heat, Jamie and I step into a downtown bookstore. The air is surgically chilled. The store is quiet. They have complimentary benches where we can park our flabby, giant, American assumptions. I shed my backpack and tell the math teacher I'm going to look around to find a book, maybe buy a bottle of water.

I ask the cashier whether they have any *"libros en Inglés."*

The man behind the counter will not even look at me.

"Hello?" I say.

Nothing.

"Can you hear me?" I say in Spanish.

The man will not even acknowledge me.

He is dressed in a Gucci sweater, with oddly shaped purple geometric eyeglasses, wearing a gel-intensive modern hairstyle that looks like his head has been dipped in Thousand Island dressing and lit with an acetylene blowtorch.

I repeat my question.

No answer.

"*Perdón*," I say. "I know you can hear me."

The man still pretends like I am invisible.

So I smile and jingle the change in my pockets. I am not leaving this store without at least being acknowledged. This is the rudest I can remember being treated outside of a Southern Baptist business meeting.

I ask my question again.

"Do you have any books in English?"

He rolls his eyes.

Then the man sighs as though it pains him to do so. He lazily points to a small shelf, two feet in length, and tells me these are the only English books they have. And please hurry up and make my selection because he has things to do.

I smile again.

"Thank you."

The bookshelf contains only American children's books. But these are desperate times, so I purchase the most adultish book they have, which is *Harry Potter and the Philosopher's Stone*. Also, I buy a fourth-grade retelling of *Oliver Twist*. My choice in literature does not endear me to my new cashier friend. He looks at the colorful kiddy books I place onto the counter, then raises an eyebrow.

His eyes meet mine.

"*Oliver Twist?*"

"I like the pictures," I say.

He handles the books like he is handling containers of bodily fluid. He covers his nose a few times, winces, and clears his throat, just to let me know that I am foul.

I take my receipt. I look him in the eye and say, "God bless you."

My wife hoists her backpack.

"And the horse you rode in on, sir," she adds.

THE MATH TEACHER AND I CHANGE OUR MINDS ABOUT staying in Burgos. We are not going to spend the night in Snobbsville. I've been kicked out of fancier cities than this. So we keep walking.

As it turns out, the Camino is extremely poorly marked in Burgos. And by "poorly marked," I mean "unmarked in many places." Our spotty phone service is pooping out, and GPS is not working. Normally this wouldn't be a problem, we'd just follow the yellow arrows that are *everywhere* in Spain. The yellow arrows on a blue background are on every edifice, embedded in every cobblestone street, inlaid in the pavement.

But in Burgos, we can't find many arrows.

What is going on here?

The few we *do* find are hidden, as though we are on a scavenger hunt. We have hiked two hundred miles of Camino over the last weeks, across the Pyrenees Mountains, crossing rivers, ascending impossible cliff faces; never once did we lose the trail. But here in Burgos, we are helplessly confused. We get lost so badly at one point that we discover we are walking *backward* on the Camino. I didn't think this was even possible. I'm starting to think Burgos doesn't like pilgrims very much.

But then again, I might be overthinking this because I'm exhausted. Also, people fanning the air when I pass them isn't putting me in a great mood.

The math teacher and I walk in relative silence, searching for arrows that will guide us out of this place. Finally, after an hour, we find our way out of town. When we exit Burgos, my wife shakes the dust off her boots and guzzles from a bottle of water.

"*Harry Potter?*" she says. "Really?"

WE FIND OURSELVES ALONE ON THE TRAIL FOR SEVERAL miles. Nobody else is out here. Just the cicadas, screaming for mercy in the Spanish heat. All the pilgrims have bedded down for the night, but we're still out here.

In hindsight, we probably should've stayed in Burgos. It would've been the smart thing to do. But I let my ego get the best of me, and now I'm paying for it. Too poor to paint, too proud to whitewash.

S.D.

Although it's late, the sun is somehow getting even hotter. How is this even possible? Sundown doesn't occur until around 9:30 p.m. in this country, and I am perishing in this heat. How do people live here? And more importantly, *why* do they live here?

We take shelter beneath a tree, and I am feeling dizzy.

"I have to stop walking," I tell the math teacher.

"We have to keep going," she says.

"I know. But I need a second."

"Look around. There is nowhere to *take* a second."

She is right. There are no trees. Only dirt and more flat earth.

I plop down beside a highway guardrail. I fan myself with my cowboy hat. Then I close my eyes. I just want to sleep. I need to sleep. That's how hot I am. I feel sick. My wife, filled with what can only be called "the warmth of maternal compassion," begins throwing rocks at me.

"Stop," I say.

Another tiny rock hits me on the lower lip.

"That hurts," I say.

The next stone catches my ear.

"If you don't stop doing that . . ."

"Quit being a wuss."

"I'm serious, Jamie."

"Wussy."

"I mean it, dammit."

"Wuss 'n' Boots."

So we keep walking.

By the time we hit the village of Tardajos, we have been walking under the relentless Iberian sun for a total of nine hours straight. I definitely don't feel good. This is starting to seem dangerous. Even the math teacher is now nauseous.

Tardajos is a town made of stone and stucco. Itty-bitty. And ancient. We pass an old woman as we are hobbling into the village. She, too, is hobbling. So we hobble together for a little bit.

She smiles. *"Que tal, peregrinos?"* ("How are you, pilgrims?")

"Nosotros olemos," I replied. ("We stink.")

The woman laughs. *"Si. Yo sé."* ("You're telling me, pal.")

"*Hay un mercado en los alrededores?*" ("Is there a market nearby?")

She points. "*Sí.*" ("Are you blind, cowboy?")

"*Gracias.*"

"*Nada.*"

We visit the store for provisions. The door dings when we enter. The math teacher and I almost collapse from sheer depletion. Everyone in the store is looking at us. But we are too overheated to care. I sit directly on the floor to keep from passing out. The math teacher is leaning against the wall, eyes closed.

The air is cool. The linoleum is even cooler. There are coolers full of cold drinks and popsicles galore. I decide I am going to eat every popsicle in this place if it kills me.

The *tienda* is an old-school general store. A mom-and-pop deal. There are canned goods on the walls. A deli case up front. The owner stands attentively behind the counter and seems genuinely glad to see us.

"*Peregrinos!*" she says, opening her arms. "Please, rest. Rest!"

She comes to me. I am covered in sweat and dust. My skin is weathered and burnt. I know I must repulse her, but she never shows it. She gives me bottled water. She gives me bread. She touches my face, like a mother. She speaks sweet, soft, whispered words of encouragement.

"Rest, *peregrino*. Rest. I am here."

We are not pleasant to behold. And yet the proprietor seems so happy to see us. So happy that we have chosen to visit her store. Even though hers is the only store we can find in Tardajos, she is acting as though she is honored by our presence. Soon I am on my feet again. The woman is cheerful. She is cracking jokes and making conversation and just generally being the nicest human being I've ever met.

So is everyone else in this store. The local customers shopping in the market even insist that we check out first, although they were all in line ahead of us. We are *peregrinos*, they tell us, with reverent voices. As if this means that we are somehow more than foolish Americans with expensive backpacks.

It isn't long before everyone in the store is involved in small talk, asking where we are from, taking a genuine interest in our journey on the Camino. I am doing my best to speak Spanish, but I am heavy-tongued from exhaustion. So everyone makes a great effort to speak English, to help us pilgrims feel at home. These people are so neighborly, so attentive, so generous, that my longtime belief is reinforced: small towns really are inherently kinder than big cities.

Before we leave, almost everyone in the store takes a moment to shake our hands and sincerely wish us "Buen Camino." These are ordinary locals, with nothing to gain from us, and yet they are treating us so much nicer than we were treated in Burgos. As I am leaving, the shopkeeper woman emerges from the store to chase me down. She is bearing a box of popsicles.

She hands them to me. "Is for you," she says.

"No," I say. "I don't need this many popsicles."

"Take them, *peregrino*."

"At least let me pay you for them."

She shakes her head. "No, *peregrino*. You do not pay for this."

I am overcome.

"What a wonderful village," I remark to an old man who is sitting on the sidewalk who looks faintly like Anthony Quinn.

"No," the man replies in a graveled voice. "What a wonderful world, *peregrino*."

VERY DAY IS THE SAME. YOU WAKE UP; YOU WALK. Eat, sleep, walk. Repeat. This is your life now.

A long time ago you did other things in your life. But that life is gone. Just a distant dream. You were another person back then. Your life now is only about walking.

Also, you do a lot of looking for cheesecake. You are always hunting for cheesecake. You've learned that Spain has the best cheesecake in the known solar system. "Burnt Basque cheesecake," they call it. And it's everywhere. In every café and bar. And you can afford to eat all the cheesecake your little hind parts desire because you are walking upward of fifteen miles per day. If you want cheesecake for breakfast, lunch, and dinner you can have it. That's the point you're at now. You feel the same way about beer.

Amazingly, you like to walk. You *really* like it, actually. It's fun. Traveling to different villages expressly by the power of your own legs. On your own feet. All this walking is vaguely reminiscent of your childhood, bringing back memories from when you used to walk to school. Back in the days when American grade school students walked to school, through rain, sleet, and snow, uphill, both ways, while carrying their little brothers on their backs.

Still, after a few weeks, the newness of walking has worn off. And you realize you are basically a homeless person. You have nowhere to live. You are always moving. Always dirty. Always ripe smelling. Always going to the bathroom in places you never imagined, some of which do not feature a toilet at all but are, in fact, abandoned utility sheds with a single hole in the floor.

Once the newness wears off, your walk is officially beginning.

The next stages of the Camino tax your mind. Not the body, but the delicate mental muscle between the ears. This is where your Camino actually begins. All the hiking you've done up until this moment has all been research. Now you're a real pilgrim.

Sometimes, for example, you find yourself in need of directions to your albergue or a market to buy food. Sometimes you are confused, and your phone GPS doesn't work. So you resort to common begging. Begging for directions. Begging for information. Begging for a sliver of someone's attention. This is beyond humbling, to be helpless in a foreign place. To be deaf, dumb, and unable to communicate. You approach strangers in the streets with your hat, literally, in your hands.

Other times you and your wife are sitting outside a church's open doorway, half asleep, covered in mud. Your cowboy hat is off, resting at your feet. Then a family of sightseeing European tourists enter the church. They are speaking French and traveling through Spain to see all the sights. The dad of the family sees you lying in the doorway. He sees your hat. He sees the holes in your clothes. He digs into his pocket and tosses pocket change into your upside-down hat.

"I'm not homeless," you explain to this man.

But he does not speak English. He thinks you're asking for more money, so he puts a few more euros into your hat. You don't even bother to correct him this time. At this point, you just accept the money and ask if he knows where you can find cheesecake.

The most testing part of it all, however, is not the walking.

It's not the begging. It's not even the confusion. It's the albergues.

Albergues are your greatest blessing and your fiercest trial. They are the heartbeat of your trail community. The social center. The albergue is your only home. An albergue is a communal bunk facility where, according to European Union laws, at least eight out of ten guests must suffer from life-threatening obstructive sleep apnea.

You had no idea how many people, globally, were apnea victims until now. You used to think sleep apnea wasn't that big of a deal. You used to believe the threat of nuclear war was the main international issue in the world. But now you know the biggest crisis facing humanity is definitely sleep apnea. It's hard to slumber through the night without using expletives.

Then a rooster crows.

There is always a rooster in the immediate vicinity of all albergues. This is also European law. Goodness knows Spain loves their roosters. They are everywhere. Sometimes they strut right down main street, eating bugs. But you would gladly listen to a warehouse full of crowing roosters if it meant that you never heard snoring again.

And so, each morning, you keep walking. You walk before the sun has fully risen. Sometimes a negative thought enters your brain. Like the thought that even though you have been out here for weeks, covered hundreds of miles, you're *still* not even halfway to Santiago. And then you see something ahead. Off to the side of the trail stands a sign reaching at least ten feet above your head. It's a fun sign with graphics, showing the route to Santiago in picture form. And judging by the location of the cute little walking man on the giant map, it looks like you have roughly six million miles remaining.

That's when it becomes real.

"Look at this," you are saying to your wife in mock disbelief. "Look how far we have to go." There is dread in your voice.

It's not that you're unsure whether you can keep doing this. Of course you know it's possible to finish this trail. The human body can do all sorts of remarkable things. But why suffer?

Why sleep in rural, rundown albergues that make an average Motel 6 look like the White House? Why listen to all this snoring, night in and night out? Why get bedbugs? Why are you doing this to yourself? What are you gaining from this?

There are the spiritual reasons, of course. You keep reminding yourself that spirituality is your primary motivation for being here. You've already been freed of a few significant burdens. You've already had a few moments of clarity.

There's the "people" reason, of course. You've already shared the most incredible communion with other humans. You've already hugged more human beings in two weeks than you've hugged in your entire life.

There is a miracle reason too. You're moved to tears every few hours hearing about the miracles that have taken place for other pilgrims. You haven't personally witnessed a miracle yet. But you're definitely more open to this idea than you've ever been before. Namely because the Trail-Miracle Ratio is *much* higher than the Daily-Life-Miracle Ratio. Why? Probably because you're paying attention now.

We pilgrims are here for all these things, I guess. That's our reason. That's why we suffer. We are here to find love. To find proof of miracles. We are here for this shining community of people who are looking for the same things. We are here for discomfort, which pushes us closer into each other. We are even here for the snoring. But when you boil it all down, mostly, we are just here for the cheesecake.

I CROSS MYSELF AND TAKE A PEW.

The ancient church is small and silent. There are a few pilgrims praying, kneeling on the stone floor. No prayer benches. Just knees against cold stone. There are candles. Lots of religious artwork on the walls.

After eight hours of daily walking beneath a wickedly hot sun, you learn to love churches. You love them on a more human level, appreciating them for exactly what they are. Shelter.

This church is a tiny one. Maybe the tiniest I've seen on the Camino so far. You don't see many little churches on the Camino. Most churches in this country are Gothic cathedrals, national monuments, stone gargantuan wonders, with huge bells, towering medieval wooden doors, and arresting golden altars. This isn't one of those places. This is a small rock-and-mortar chapel, squatting by the roadside. It looks more like an old barn than a church. You'd miss it if you weren't looking for it.

There is a nun by the door, smiling at visitors as they enter. She is small, wearing thick nylons, practical shoes, and a navy-blue habit.

I sit before the altarpiece. I bow my head.

Ironically, at this exact moment I am here, Pope Francis's funeral is taking place, thousands of miles from this dusty pueblo, in Rome. All day, pilgrims on the trail have been watching the funeral proceedings via cell phone. His funeral is a major world event, and the Camino is indirectly connected

with this. Everyone out there is interested. And so, right now as I rest in this chapel, in the Vatican City, there are kings, queens, magistrates, lawmakers, prime ministers, and presidents in attendance. There are a hundred and thirty national delegations, fifty heads of state, and four thousand journalists from around the world, scrupulously covering the critical world event so they may report on internationally important details, such as what outfit the US president is wearing.

But these little nuns are not thinking about the Vatican City. They do not care about geopolitical posturing or any politician's outfit. They are here, in the tranquil village of Rabé de las Calzadas, tending to pilgrims. They are focused on the here and now. Do you need a bottle water, pilgrim? Do you need prayer? Do you need anything? May I bless you?

I am dirty, weathered. I am tired of my own smell. I have been walking eight hours, and I am weary from heat, heavy backpacks, and plain monotony.

I am staring at the altar. And I'm feeling tired all over. I am tired of sleeping in bunks with all the sounds of throat clearing, nose blowing, and nocturnal flatulations that could shake plaster from the ceilings. I'm tired of never knowing whether my shower stall will be gross. I'm tired of never knowing whether we will even *have* accommodations for the evening. I'm tired of the constant pressure I feel when communicating with people whose language I am so terrible at speaking.

What is this *really* all about? What is my *why*? Everyone has a why. Every pilgrim has some reason they are doing this. I've never quite identified my why. What am I seeking? I've asked myself this a hundred times, but the answer never comes.

Maybe I am here because I am the same age as my father was when he took his own life. Maybe I am here because the night before his death, he tried to kill my mother and me, and I live with that every day.

Perhaps I am here because my father held my sister and me hostage until the sheriff's department arrived with riot guns and subdued him, and I have never been able to unsee this. Or it could be that I am here because the last image of my father was his arrest. Maybe I am here because I almost shot my own father with a hunting rifle. I have lived with these traumas. I have let them ruin my health. Ruin my mind. Ruin my relationships. Ruin me. I have let trauma make me afraid. I have locked myself in a prison of my own fear and swallowed the key.

Maybe I am here because I dropped out of school. Or because I never even knew my father's family, who disowned us after his death. Who wrote us out of the will. It might be that I am here because we struggled financially when I was a kid. I have spent the majority of my life dealing with my own moderate mental illness, grappling with depression until my late twenties. I had nightmares until I was thirty. My life has been an embarrassment to me. It humiliates me.

Maybe I am here because sometimes I grieve for the little boy I used to be. That little, innocent boy who could do nothing but pity himself. Sometimes I want to put that tragic little boy to rest and let him lie in peace, alongside the remains of my father's Great Mistake. I want to say goodbye to that little boy forever. I don't want to be him anymore. I want to be the person I've always wanted to be. I do not want to be shackled to that little boy's past anymore. I just want to be free.

I want a new life. I want a new mind. I want a new heart. I want a new start.

The small nun shuffles to me.

I feel awkward because I am afraid she's going to tell me I've been sitting here too long and it's time for me to leave. She is elderly and walks with toddling steps. The sister speaks to me in Spanish and doesn't expect a dorky American pilgrim like me to return her words in Spanish, so she is pleased when she learns I can understand her foreign tongue. When she realizes I can speak Spanish, I feel like I've scored some kind of point.

"Do you need prayer, my child?" she says in her language.

I tell her, yes, I think I would like someone to pray for me.

"Do you suffer?" she asks.

I pause.

I've never truly thought about it in those terms per se. Do I suffer? Yes, I tell her, I do suffer. I have been suffering for a long time, I guess. Suffering. That's exactly what I'd call it.

I am not prepared for her to move inward and embrace me the way she does. The imaginary walls come down between us. She is in my space now. I am not prepared for a tiny Spanish woman to grasp my face in both hands and press her small forehead against mine. Her hands are hot. The skin of her face is soft and sticky. I can feel the bone of her brow against my own. She smells like verbena. She is gentle. Like a favorite aunt. Or like the grandmother I always wanted. She holds me like this for a few moments without speaking. Our two foreheads, pressed together.

Soon, I am crying like a teenage girl. Other pilgrims are staring at me. Look at the big, stupid American, sobbing and making a spectacle of himself. But I can't help it. I suffer.

She prays.

"Padre nuestro, que estás en el cielo . . ."

The prayer lasts for a long time. She finishes the recited prayers and begins blessing me. I can tell she is making the words up as she goes. She is merely talking to God, just like

I'm talking to you now, asking him to bless me. She tells him to give me everything I need. To set me free. To give me newness of life. To show me how deeply I am loved. To show me how deeply I have always been loved.

When she finishes, she gently traces the sign of the cross on my forehead using her thumb. After which we just hug some more, rocking back and forth, while other pilgrims give us space. We stay like that for a long time. Until the tears stop. When I leave the chapel, my backpack seems lighter somehow.

And so it was that on April 26, 2025, Pope Francis was laid to rest.

And so, I believe, was that sad little boy.

TODAY THE POWER WENT OUT IN SPAIN. NOT JUST some of Spain. All of Spain. There is no power in Spain right now. Spain is in the Dark Ages.

At first, we did not know the power was out, of course. The only thing any of us noticed while walking the remote trail was that our phones had stopped working. Which is not unusual on the Camino. Out here, your American-carrier phone service only works on days of the week beginning with R or Z. But when we arrived in the hamlet of Carrión de los Condes, however, we realized something was indeed very wrong. Our phones were in emergency mode, and we couldn't pull up any maps to find our albergue.

And so we wander the serpentine route into Carrión de los Condes proper, where all the locals are hanging out, seated outside their respective buildings, seemingly without a care in the world. Nobody appears bothered by the absence of electricity. Carrión de los Condes is an old village. They spent the first several hundred years without power. This isn't anything new.

"Notice anything weird," the math teacher says.

"Yeah, nobody is playing on their phones."

Kids are playing *fútbol* in the street. People are sitting on curbs, having animated conversations over midday bottles of wine. Everyone is eating ice cream cones. I guess everyone's ice cream is going to thaw and be ruined anyway. Lick 'em if you got 'em.

People play cards on tables outside cafés. It is dusk, but there are no lights anywhere. All the shops are open; all the shop owners stand on the sidewalks, listlessly smoking cigarettes, blue haze gathering around their heads, staring into space.

I find a small older man sitting on the stoop of his townhouse, sipping what looks like coffee from a thimble-size glass.

"Excuse me, sir," I ask in Spanish. "Is the power off?"

"*Sí*," he replies.

"In all of Carrión de los Condes? Or in all of Spain."

"*Sí.*"

"*Sí?* You mean, in all of Spain?"

"*Sí.*"

"A nationwide power outage?" says the math teacher.

"*Sí*," he replies.

"Do you happen to know the reason for the outage, or how long it will last?"

He shrugs.

"Has your power been off all day?"

"*Sí.*"

There is a tiny elderly woman behind him who is watering a flower box. She is a round woman with silver hair, and she's wearing an apron.

"Is that your wife?" I ask.

"*Sí.*"

"What's her name?"

"*Sue.*"

The wife is more of a conversationalist than her better half. She tells me that her radio reported an "*apogo de energía en todo España*" ("a nationwide power outage"). Nobody has any more information than this, she explains as she slowly begins watering her begonias again.

The man's wife gives us directions to our albergue and does not seem in the least bit bothered by the outage. Which is astounding to me. I grew up in Florida. During each hurricane season, our power would go out all the time. We experienced mass outages for weeks on end. And I can tell you this: Americans handle an outage with a *very* different attitude. We raid supermarkets for bread, milk, and Clorox. Americans are obsessed with bleach during hurricanes.

But nobody in Carrión de los Condes really seems to give a flying fig that there is no power. Most of their stores and homes don't have A/C anyway. And hey, they don't mind using flashlights. We visit a market for supplies and food for supper. The employees are standing on the street, handing out flashlights for customers to use, like it's no big deal. My wife and I buy canned food for supper and one fresh baguette about as big as a grown woman's thigh. We will have no means of cooking since our albergue kitchen is electric, but a fresh baguette covers a multitude of sins.

I am marveling at how easygoing everyone seems. A power outage in the US is a tense time. We Americans would constantly be listening to updates on battery-powered radios, grilling all the meat in our fridges, and the anxious "vibe" in the air would be vaguely reminiscent of a Soviet invasion. But here in the far-off regions of rural Spain, it's post-siesta-thirty, and everybody is well-rested and has a strong wine buzz going.

For supper, we sit around the albergue table, drinking warm beer, eating cold *alubias* (beans) and *pan* (bread), gazing out an open window overlooking the stone streets of Carrión. Children are playing below. We are serenaded by their happy voices and swells of laughter. I see some boys horsing around with local dogs. Young girls are playing what looks like tag.

When supper is finished, we take cold showers that are icy enough to shrink our skin and damage a few of our gender-specific external organs. Then I open my fiddle case, rosin my bow, and begin to tune. I play a few melodies while sitting near the window, overlooking the mismatched rooflines of terra-cotta tiles and the acres of aluminum TV antennas.

A grade-school boy on the street below stands and stares up at me, evidently transfixed by the sound of my fiddle. His little friends gather around him. One is carrying a ball beneath his arm. They are all staring upward at me with huge grins. When I finish playing, they all shout, "*Bravo! Bravissimo! Vaya!*" And they applaud. An old woman passing by joins the group of youthful onlookers. The woman looks up, listens for a little bit, and then gave me a hearty "*Oye!*" A young man riding a bike stops pedaling and joins my growing clot of spectators. Soon, there is a miniature audience listening to me fiddle. People on the street begin dancing. The old woman can really shake it.

This is surreal. Is this really happening?

After a few songs, the day is over. The sun has set, and

without electric lamps, you have no choice but to sleep. I put the fiddle away. The last few spears of orange sun fade behind the church spire of San Andres Cathedral. In the final minutes of dusk, I bid farewell to the day at hand by reading *Harry Potter* while nibbling on a bar of French chocolate. My wife is journaling in her notebook. The air is cool and pleasant, smelling faintly of cedar, livestock, and thyme. And I am thinking to myself that it's downright amazing what you find yourself doing when your precious handheld devices quit working. You start living.

"I hope the power never comes back on," says the math teacher.

"*Bravo,*" says I.

ORNING. A BAR, SOMEWHERE IN RURAL SPAIN. A rooster is crowing near the open door. Distant goats are bleating. Old, stout, thick-handed farmers gather to chew the morning fat. There are pilgrims eating breakfast, clothed in wicking apparel, weary from traversing half a nation, with thinned rubber soles beneath their feet.

There is a television in the corner of the bar broadcasting the morning *noticias*. The news stations in Spain are a lot like the news stations in the US, offering your morning dose of adrenaline and terror. Nothing they have to say is positive or uplifting. The world is going to hell. Details after this commercial break. The one thing they don't have in this country are televised pharmaceutical advertisements. Such ads are illegal here.

Beneath the television is a lineup of heavy backpacks, all belonging to pilgrims, loaded with the weight of the world. Alongside the Osprey, North Face, and REI packs stands a forest of telescopic hiking poles.

The old farmers at the bar are speaking rapid-fire Spanish, drinking tall beers with their morning croissants and breakfast cheesecake. These rural Europeans live too loosely, free from the evangelical rules that govern our society. They drink beer with breakfast, wolf down cheesecake at sunup, smoke cigars without remorse, and nap away their precious afternoon hours. How sad to think of the multitudes in this beautiful country who have gone to their graves and never knew there was hell.

"*Díme*," the bartender says to me.

I order a *café con leche*. The old man next to me is smoking a small cigar. He offers me one. I have never been one to turn down the kindness of strangers. He lights my cigar with a match and introduces himself.

"*C'est bon, non?*" he says.

"*Oui*," I say, demonstrating the only French word I know.

I am awaiting my coffee while watching TV. The newscaster is talking about Spain's nationwide power outage. Everyone in the bar is either engrossed in a newspaper or focused on the television. We are all very interested in the news because these updates affect us personally. Many of us are visitors here. We are all from distant countries, dependent on the charity of each other. Also, we have already heard horror stories about pilgrims who were stranded in bigger cities during the recent power outage.

We heard about one young pilgrim in León who slept on the street during the blackout. Other pilgrims found him shivering against an alley wall. He'd been beaten and robbed by hoodlums. That same night, the high-school-age pilgrims joined him, all sleeping in a huddle to keep warm and safe. They bandaged his wounds and pooled their money for him to stay at a local hotel until he was healed enough to resume his Camino.

There was another story about a large group of pilgrims who were stuck on a train for an entire day. They had almost no food, so they all met together in the dining car and combined their food scraps and supplies to make supper. They all ate and were satisfied, and they collected twelve baskets of leftovers.

There are other stories too. These tales are passed from

pilgrim to pilgrim along the Camino; news travels purely by word of mouth out here. They call this the "Camino Telegraph." You find yourself invested in people's lives out here. All it takes is one conversation, and you love them deeply.

The old man next to me has a white beard. His skin is shoe leather. He looks like a cross between Moses and a hobbit. You can tell he is a pilgrim because he smells like the rest of us. He has a heavy French accent, but he can speak English. The left half of his face is paralyzed. There is a string of rosary beads dangling from his pocket.

He removes the cigar from his mass of facial hair and tells me this is his seventh Camino.

"Seventh?" I say.

"*Oui*. I first hiked the Camino after I died, many years ago."

Everyone is silent.

"Died?" says the bartender. "*You* died?"

"*Oui*."

At first we aren't sure we heard him correctly.

Roberto, a Catholic priest from Brazil, seated on my other side, is obviously perplexed.

"You're saying you died?" Roberto says, adjusting his glasses and taking a long look at the old man.

I can tell what Roberto is thinking. I am thinking the same. This old man looks plenty alive. And he definitely smells alive.

The old man tells a story. When he was in his forties, he died for several minutes. His death wasn't on an operating table. It wasn't in a hospital bed. He says he was on the toilet, of all places. He had a stroke. He collapsed. And thus began an ethereal experience that changed his entire perspective on life itself.

"What happened?" Roberto asks.

The old man says he exited his body, floating high above it. He watched paramedics stuff his body into a body bag. He saw himself being carried out of his apartment. He saw it all, from outside himself.

After that, a glowing woman appeared to him. She was made of light. She was lovely. And she looked like his late mother. She whisked him away into a world of whiteness. This was something he wanted us to understand clearly. He kept saying everything was light.

"*Tout était lumière*," says the old man. "Everywhere, there is light."

"Light?" Roberto asks.

The old man nods. "Inside and outside. Light."

By now, several other pilgrims at the bar are leaning inward to listen. The old man offers them all cigars until he has no more left. The air is nothing but silvery haze as he speaks.

So there he was, in this great whiteness. There, he saw mountains and trees and streams and flowers. And strangely, he felt unified with each tree and flower and rock. He could even communicate with them. All the flowers, for example, knew him by name. And he knew them by name. And whenever he walked through this flowery field, the flowers all moved aside, yielding to make a path for him. He could travel incredible distances, just by pointing to a mountaintop or a hillside, whereupon his body would instantly arrive there.

"And colors," the old man says. "I could see more colors than there are words to describe the colors." He tapped his ash. "Our human eyes, they cannot see even one percent of the color spectrum, did you know that? There are colors in the next world that do not exist here."

By now almost everyone in the bar is listening to him. Hardly anyone is moving as the old man speaks. He tells a story of family members whom he was reunited with, a story of forgiveness, and of the pure joy with which he was enraptured. He speaks of a movie-like life review; all his earthly events were played before his eyes, like a feature film. He speaks about meeting God, who, as it turns out, was nothing like he expected, and did not resemble Charleton Heston or Morgan Freeman. But mostly, the old man describes an overwhelming, awe-inducing, bone-crushingly intense realization of absolute lovingkindness.

"Everything is made of love," he explains. "Love is, how you say, like the atomic matter of life itself."

"Atomic matter," says the bartender.

Roberto stares into his empty beer glass. "Everything is made of love. I like that."

By the end of his story, our small group of dusty pilgrims is listening with slack jaws. Our breakfasts are cold. The ash on our cigars is long.

The old man rises from his barstool and pays his bill. He wanders outside, where he begins packing a wagon. He will pull this wagon all the way to Santiago, like a draft horse. Just like he did the first six times. This is his seventh wagon. The cart contains a tent, food, water, clothing, cookware, replacement shoes, first-aid kits, and of course, red wine. There is a dog sleeping beside his wagon. He calls the dog by name. The dog leaps to its feet and wags its tail.

He checks the tarp covering his cart and tightens the strap that hold the tarp in place. Then he lifts the handles of the wagon and secures them to a belt attached to his waist. Like a mule wearing a harness.

"Love," the old man says, "is the glue that binds all things. Love is the empty space between all objects. There is no death, only love. Even our mistakes are made of love, for they continually point us toward forgiveness, which is also love."

The old man pauses to light another cigar. "I was given a choice, you know."

"What kind of choice?" the priest asks.

"I was told that if I came back to earth, life would be very hard for me because of my stroke. I was told there would be pain. But still, I chose to leave that wonderful realm and come back here."

"Why?" says a young woman pilgrim. "Why would anyone ever leave?"

The old man smiles. "Oh, *ma petite*. Because I have a message to share."

"What message?" I ask.

The old man smiles again. "You just heard it."

*L*EÒN CATHEDRAL IS AMONG THE GREATEST OF HUman works in Gothic style. This cathedral was the first monument ever declared in Spain back in 1844. It is one of this country's most precious relics. The French-influenced architectural masterpiece is simply known as the *Casa de la Luz*, the House of Light. This is because the church features one of the world's largest collections of medieval stained-glass windows. The brilliant thirteenth-century glass mosaics reach high into the heavens, depicting biblical scenes with arresting color.

History is everywhere in Spain. On every corner. In every crevice. Within every stone. Don't get me wrong, we have a lot of history in America too. Many of our historic buildings date all the way back to the mid-1940s. But here in Spain, when you touch stonework from the Dark Ages, when you feel the weight of medieval plank doors beneath your hands, when you view stained glasswork that is three times as old as your own nation, history takes on a different feeling.

Right now, the bells of León are ringing, calling the people to Mass. You can hear the bells toll across the city on this rainy morning, cutting through rain showers that fall on León like large quilts of mist. I am wearing my waterproof boots, trotting across the wet town square, splashing through puddles, just in time for church.

People are swarming around the cathedral like ants around a Snickers bar. It seems that everyone in the Western world is attending Mass today. The church is full. There are no pews available. I stand in the rear of the ornate sanctuary alongside other pilgrims who stand. Our five-hundred-pound backpacks snugly fitted upon our shoulders.

Daylight shines through a stone Gothic frame of a hundred and thirty individual stained-glass windows, illuminating the heads of all the congregants with a spectrum of ancient colors. It's like being inside a rainbow. Many of the walls inside the cathedral have been deconstructed and replaced with all glass to allow for maximum light. So this really is the House of Light.

Mass is conducted in Spanish. Although I am only able to understand a total of three words, as the priest's speech is obscured by echoes. He is speaking way too fast for the acoustics of this room.

I look around. The nave, the north aisle, and the south aisle are full of pilgrims this morning. There are hundreds of us here. Mass at León is a rite of passage for pilgrims, no matter what your religion. There are more pilgrims filtering in through the doors. This room cannot hold any more people. I wonder if they have fire marshals in Spain.

It hurts to stand this morning. I am currently nursing a spasmed calf muscle. It is only a cramp, I think. But it has slowed me down considerably over these past few days. I am now walking with a slight limp, lingering behind the rest of the hikers. As a result of slower walking, I am spending even more time on my feet, which only aggravates the cramping. Walks that should take me five hours are now taking seven and eight. For the last several miles, other pilgrims have been passing me. They see the telltale athletic tape on my calf and ask in concerned voices, *"Estas bien?"*

"Bien, bien," I always reply with a self-effacing laugh.

Deep inside I am embarrassed. Because I feel like a fool out here. Limping along, surrounded by teens and twenty-somethings who trot circles around me. But I don't want to talk about my pain this morning. Talking about it causes it to be more present in my thoughts. I just want to finish this trail.

Most of the pilgrims in this sanctuary are young. There are many teenage hikers in the pews directly in front of me. They are brimming with adolescent energy, emitting sine waves of testosterone and estrogen in this sanctuary. They are strong and fit. Young and attractive. So hopelessly optimistic about life and all its possibilities. So obviously unaware of all they don't know. Youth is a potent hallucinogenic.

I feel three times their age this morning. I also feel like a consummate ass. I don't often think of myself as an old guy—I'm *not* an old guy. But when I am around the kids on this trail, I feel like Grandpa Jones. They call me sir. They realize I'm old enough to be their dad, and they treat me like it. And they aren't wrong. There is a huge age gap between us. They stay up until the wee hours, pulling all-nighters, laughing and guzzling beer until the sun comes up. Whereas I'm at the age when an "all-nighter" means not having to wake up to pee more than three times in a row.

The injury is starting to aggravate me, standing here in the rear of the sanctuary, listening to Mass recited by Charlie Brown's schoolteacher. And with each throb of shin pain, I am trying not to wince. I want to sit. I need to sit. But all the pews are taken by the cast of *Barney and Friends*.

My eyes are drawn to the stained-glass image that is directly above me.

I assume I am looking at the apostle Peter. You can usually tell which one is Peter. Peter is generally the apostle who looks like Jerry Garcia. He is almost always drawn by artists as a big, lovable, moderately dumb, uncoordinated, hairy guy. He stands with eleven other bearded Dead Heads, all wearing bathrobes and Birkenstocks. They are looking back at me with the obligatory biblical frowns on their faces.

As I stare at this window, I find myself wishing that I could understand what the priest is saying. Maybe his words could inspire me. Perhaps, if I could only understand his words, I might find the wherewithal to face today's shin pain.

"Please, let me understand," I whisper beneath my breath.

Then something happens. The priest makes eye contact with me. He stops talking for a brief moment. Then he resumes his talking, but this time it seems like he is speaking slower. Then again, maybe my ears are simply adjusting to the cadence of his words. Either way, he sounds less like a livestock auctioneer and more like a preacher. I am now able to understand what he is saying.

This excites me, somewhat. I lean over to my friend Noam and whisper, "Did he just slow down?"

"What?" says Noam.

Noam is a nineteen-year-old from Israel, a devout Hasidic Jew, wearing a *kippah* on his head. He is dry-humored and mostly quiet. He has never attended a Catholic Mass in his life, and says his mother would murder him if she found out. Not figurative murder, he explains, but the actual ten-o'clock-news kind of murder.

I whisper, "I can actually understand the priest's words now."

Noam stares at me flatly. "Mazel tov."

The priest is reading scripture, reciting a story about the apostle Peter from the final chapters of the book of John. In the story, Jesus is newly resurrected. Peter and the guys are fishing in a boat when they see Jesus standing on the shoreline. When Peter sees Jesus, he screams, "It's the Lord!" Then he dives into the water. He swims ashore like the impulsive, reckless rocket scientist that he is. It's a long way to the shore. But he swims the full distance. Have you ever tried swimming a quarter mile? It's a wonder that Peter doesn't drown. But he doesn't drown; he makes it. Then he crawls out of the water, sopping wet, and he probably hugs Jesus, because this is what impulsive rocket scientists do.

Soon, they are all sitting around a campfire. Peter is probably cold and wet, and Jesus is definitely going to have to take his resurrection tunic to the dry cleaners. They are cooking breakfast, laughing, hanging out. And that's when Jesus asks Peter if he loves him.

Peter replies, yes, of course he loves him. Of course, Lord.

Where have you been? I just swam a quarter mile.

Then Jesus asks him again, "Do you love me?"

And Peter answers yes again.

Jesus asks this question a third time.

This time Peter is deeply hurt.

Peter says, "You *know* I love you, Lord."

And it occurs to me that there are probably tears in Peter's eyes when he answers, because only days earlier, Peter saw Jesus bound in chains, led away to his execution. Peter probably felt powerless to help his friend at the time. He was outnumbered. He couldn't fight them off. Anything Peter did would have resulted in his own death.

And so, as Jesus was being flogged by his captors, his best friends scattered. And for good reason too. The same jerks who captured Jesus were probably aiming to take down his disciples as well.

So Peter is on the run, trying hard to blend into his surroundings and not draw attention to himself. Trying to lay low. When all of a sudden, there are some people who recognize him. They're pot-stirrers. They're trying to pick a fight. They tell Peter they've seen him with Jesus. But Peter says, no, you're mistaken, sorry, I've never met the guy. Yes, you were, they say. You were with him, we saw you. Sorry, Peter replies, you're mixing me up with someone else. And so he denies his best friend to save his own proverbial ass.

Preachers in every pulpit have painted Peter as a cowardly lion for this, but I disagree. I don't think Jesus blamed Peter for flying beneath the radar. It was the smart thing to do. It shows that Peter cared about his family. Peter had a wife. He had kids. He was a breadwinner. What would have been the point for Peter to die? Peter was only doing what any dad would've done.

But.

It still hurt. I don't think it hurt Jesus as much as I think Peter's words hurt Peter. This might have been Peter's lowest moment. He felt as stupid as any man has ever felt.

But now, sitting here with Jesus, Peter's friend was saying, "It's okay. We're good." Peter was being forgiven for his screwup. Three times. Publicly forgiven, three times. And I have this feeling that if Peter had screwed up three thousand times, he would've been forgiven three thousand times as well. Three thousand times three thousand times.

I don't know how this morning's story applies to me, exactly, but I have a strange sensation that it does.

I look down at my boots.

There is elastic tape wrapped tightly on my calves. Evidence of my own rocket-science genius over the past three weeks. I look up at the image of Peter, who is beaming down at me with a warm look that says he gets it. He knows what it's like to feel stupid and reckless and foolish. And as light blares through the intricate thirteenth-century stained glasswork, I can swear all the apostles are giving me a collective thumbs-up.

THE MATH TEACHER AND I LIMP INTO RABANAL del Camino on three legs. I am holding Jamie for support as we ascend the steeply inclined street into an isolated Spanish village with a population of sixty. The rock-paved hill that leads into town feels like the summit of Denali on my wounded shins. My swollen calves are akin to Popeye's forearms. Each mincing stride is accompanied by the identical grimace Sylvester Stallone wore during the final scenes of *Rocky II*.

Other pilgrims are gawking at me, watching me gimp through town. They are looking at me with horror, as though I have the plague. I half expect them to shield their faces and hold up crucifixes as I pass them by. Pilgrims are terrified of injury. They do not want to acknowledge injury, for fear that injury will suddenly leap onto them. A minor injury can end one's Camino endeavor. It can drastically alter your plans. An injury can send you back home early with a Did Not Finish certificate. So most pilgrims, naturally, prefer not to think about injury at all. Thus, if you personally happen to be injured, other pilgrims will hesitate to look at you as you hobble by, scurrying away from you before they catch your stupid.

Rest assured, I've seldom felt so stupid as I do right now, walking into Rabanal like a man who's just been shot.

This profound stupidity hit new depths earlier today when,

after trying to find a room for tonight, we discovered—you might be noticing an overarching literary theme here—there were no available rooms.

Which is nothing new, of course. Every night it is the same. Joseph and Mary enter the village, astride their donkey, and there is no room at the inn. Although in this particular story, I feel less like Joseph and more like the ass.

I cannot walk another mile.

"I need to sit," I say.

"Okay," says the math teacher.

I collapse on a bench. My legs simply cannot handle another moment of abuse. They burn like fire. And my shins are making crunching sensations whenever I wiggle the muscles. That can't be good.

"We need to find a room," the math teacher is saying.

Earlier, we had heard from other pilgrims there was a monastery nearby that would not turn people away. That's why we hiked to Rabanal in the first place. My spirits jumped at the prospect of a place to rest my legs and recline.

"The monks *can't* turn pilgrims away," said a fellow Irish pilgrim who noticed my plight. "To turn pilgrims away is against their beliefs because the monks believe *any* visitor could be Jesus."

From the bench, I remove the phone from my pocket and dial the monastery's number. I explain to the monk our situation.

"Sorry," says the monk on the phone. "We're not accepting any pilgrims currently."

"But I thought you couldn't turn anyone away?"

"Where did you hear that?"

"That's what pilgrims on the trail are saying."

"Sorry, we are not accepting pilgrims right now."

"I can do the dishes."

"Congratulations."

My wife is looking at me with big eyes, waiting to hear what the answer is. I hold up a finger.

"So you're turning me away?"

"Not exactly."

"But what if I'm the Lord?"

Silence. "What?"

"You heard me. I said, 'What if I am the Lord?'"

"Are you the Lord?"

"Don't tell anyone."

"Buen Camino, *señor.*"

So we have no place to stay. Our only other option, I suppose, is to call a taxi. Although, I don't know where the taxi would take us. Maybe the driver could take us to his house and we could sleep in his kids' bedroom.

"There is an inn ahead," says Jamie. "Let's keep walking."

I hobble up the hill, moaning with each step. The math teacher holds me for support. The embarrassment is almost too much to bear.

"I'm so sorry," I say to her.

"We need to get you off your feet."

"I'm *such* an idiot."

"Stop saying that."

"I am such an idiot."

"You're not an idiot."

"But you said I'm a wuss."

"Those aren't the same thing."

"Wuss is different than idiot?"

"Yes."

"Different how?"

"An idiot doesn't know he's a wuss."

The terracotta rooftops are bathed in the sepia tones of afternoon sunlight. The stone and brick walls are radiating warmth as we pass them. The cobblestones beneath our feet are uneven and treacherous. Other pilgrims in town are staring at the dork in the cowboy hat who is leaning on his wife and limping up the hill.

"Everyone's looking at me," I say.

"Aren't you humble?" she says.

"No, I mean it. They're all staring."

"Well, I work out."

When I meet their glares, the realization begins to land on me. I have been trying to ignore my injury for days now. I have been trying to push through the pain, but the writing is on the wall. This is the end of my Camino. There is no going forward for me. Not like this.

That's when a vehicle pulls alongside us.

THE VEHICLE'S POWER WINDOW ROLLS DOWN. IT IS AN SUV. Black. The vehicle is keeping pace alongside us as I limp. The woman at the wheel is smiling at me. She is middle-aged, pretty, with long hair. She seems almost shocked to see me.

"Are you Sean?" the driver asks in an American accent.

The math teacher and I stop walking.

"Come again?" I say.

"Sean?" the lady says. "Are you him?"

Jamie and I just look at each other.

"Sean Dietrich," the driver says again. "From Alabama."

"Honey," I say. "I think I'm dying."

"Sean Dietrich," the lady says. "Are you the writer?"

Jamie answers the woman with a smile. "Yes, this is Sean Dietrich. And I'm Jamie, his wife. Have we met before?"

The woman presents her hand through the window. "We've never met, but I know who you two are."

I am too stunned to shake the woman's hand. You could have knocked me over with an ibuprofen tablet. I'm still not one hundred percent sure that I am lucid.

I turn to Jamie. "Please promise me you'll love again when I'm gone."

The woman throws her car into park. She steps out. "I can't believe you're here in Rabanal. I knew it was you. I'm a fan of your work." Then she shakes my hand with both of hers.

Her words seem foreign to my ears. A fan of my *what*? We are in the sixty-person village of Rabanal Del Camino in the remotest regions of the Iberian Peninsula. I am not fully certain whether this town has running water, let alone bookstores with bargain book bins containing my books.

"You are a fan of my work?"

"*Sí*."

"Ma'am," I say. "Can I ask you a serious question?"

"Sure."

"Are you the Lord?"

HER NAME IS KIM. SHE IS A WRITER TOO. SHE LIVES IN RA-banal. It turns out that Kim has read my work—which only shows you how hard-up Rabanal is for literature. She knew we were walking the Camino because she had been keeping up with my daily writings online. When I told her about my injury and how we had not been able to find lodging in the area, or in surrounding areas, or in all of the European Union, Kim's only response was, "Oh, we'll *find* you a room."

And she wasn't kidding. Kim made a series of phone calls

to get the ball rolling. And the locals pitched in to find a solution. I could not believe that veritable strangers were so vested in the interest of a lone pilgrim with swollen shins. Kim called Susana, a local innkeeper and store owner who wanted to help. Susana's inn was full, but she evidently knew every innkeeper, hotel owner, shopkeeper, merchant, and human being within several hundred square miles. Also, Susana was no shrinking violet and would not take no for an answer. Susana spent the afternoon making phone calls on our behalf. She had nothing to gain from this. She just did this out of her vast reservoir of lovingkindness while I sat outside her shop, icing my shins with icepacks. I listened as Susana made phone calls, going to bat for me. I was overcome by her charity.

"I need a room for two pilgrims tonight," Susana would say into the phone. "What do they look like? Well, the *chica*, she is very pretty, with a braid, and the *chico*, he has a lot of red hair on his face, and a cowboy hat, and he cries a lot."

Pause.

"*Si*, a cowboy hat."

Another pause.

"*Si*, two pilgrims."

Longest pause.

"*Si, Americanos*. Hello? Hello, are you still there?"

Susana was amazing. She canvassed the network of local merchants and storekeepers and kept getting met with dead ends. At times it seemed like she would never find us a room. But Susana and Kim did not give up.

"Do not worry," Susana said resolutely. "I will find you a room if I have to build one with two-by-fours and nails."

And something about her tone said that she already owned a hammer.

I wanted to cry.

"Thank you," I said.

Susana punched in another phone number and began machine-gunning a conversation in Spanish with a local innkeeper. The innkeeper said she was full, but I could translate enough to decipher that Susana was suggesting that the innkeeper move guests around, from room to room, to find us space. I could hear the innkeeper's sigh on the phone in response to this idea.

But Susana was relentless. Finally the woman put Susana on hold and said she was going to ask her boss.

Susana's face began to glow. It was the first glimmer of hope we'd had all day.

"I think they have room for you," Susana whispered, covering the mouthpiece of her phone. Then she smiled at me. "By the way, what is a *wuss*?"

M Y EYES OPEN BENEATH A QUILT-WORK OF eye boogers and grit. My head, still on the pillow. My legs are aching. My eyes first catch sight of a rosary lying on my nightstand, along with my pocketknife, a handful of pocket change, and my wallet. The rosary was given to me by the nun who blessed me in Rabé de las Calzadas, several villages back. I haven't used it because I don't know how. Mostly it's just stayed in my pocket. Sometimes I reach into my pocket and feel the beads on it and remember how much that little nun seemed to love me.

I lift the rosary and inspect it. The cross bears a hieroglyphic-like symbol on it. I have no idea what this symbol means. It looks like a very tall letter *P* with an *X* drawn through the leg. We didn't have these P-X symbols in the Baptist church. We didn't have rosaries either. The only symbols Baptists had were the blue cornflowers on your mom's CorningWare dishes.

I swing my feet and get out of bed. My shins feel like broken glass. I sit in one place cussing myself. There is no way I can walk today. I can't fathom that I'll be able to walk tomorrow either. I simply cannot conceive of walking another mile on the Camino in the shape I'm in.

I hear the noises of morning outside our room. The first thing you hear upon arising in a hostel, albergue, or inn is a choir of human sound. The symphony of morning cacophony within a Camino albergue is a concert of shuffling, thumping, squealing, thrumming, ticking, flopping, and multiple pilgrim conversations simultaneously taking place, in approximately twenty-seven thousand international languages. You hear a soprano section of backpack zippers. A tenor section of rubber soles squeaking like the girls basketball team on a gymnasium floor. A bass section of bodily orifices, clearing themselves in the form of nasal blowing, throat purging, sniffing, spitting, sneezing, coughing, grunting, moaning, and various other lower-intestinal emission sounds that Europeans don't consider a big deal. Some Europeans would have no problem making some of these explosive flatulent noises during their own wedding ceremonies.

This is our second day in Rabanal. We had to sleep somewhere different last night. I have been unable to walk for the last two days. And it isn't looking good. I've read three books, including *Harry Potter*. I've learned four new fiddle tunes. I'm merely wasting time. I've ruined our trip.

My wife is still sleeping. The sheet is pulled back, revealing her bare shoulder. I can see her brown skin showing. Her tan is deeper than most other pilgrims because of the Creek in her ancestry. She deserves to walk this Camino instead of being holed up in a hotel room. She deserves to complete what we came here to do, even if I can't.

Even so, we have become unofficial fixtures in Rabanal. In the morning the village empties itself of its current horde of pilgrims who all hit the trail. Within an hour, the town is empty. The cobbled streets are vacant, the inns evacuated. And there is nothing to do but fiddle. Which I have been doing for two days. I pick a bench on the main street and then I fiddle until the sun goes down while I watch various pilgrims wander through town. Sometimes they toss coins into my fiddle case.

I throw on my clothes. I get my fiddle case and walk downstairs to find my bench while my wife sleeps. I pass all the pilgrims who are suiting up for the day, finishing breakfasts in the dining room, bundling up to fend off the morning cold. They are so happy. They are so excited to be here. So ready to confront the obstacles of the day.

I walk outside. The air is chilled. I can see my breath. I find my bench and take a seat. I rosin my bow. I adjust my tuners. And I begin to play. The sound of the fiddle bounces down the road, ricocheting off the smooth stone walls lining the street.

If there is a more tranquil place on this side of heaven than Rabanal at six in the morning, I'd be surprised. Rabanal is a unique *pueblo*. Technically, sixty residents live here. But this is only during peak season. I am told that only thirty residents live here officially.

The origins of Rabanal del Camino date back to the eleventh century. The town's history is also linked to the Knights Templar in the Middle Ages, when soldier-monks settled this place as an outpost. The reason the knights started this town, the whole point, you could say, was to protect pilgrims who were crossing the *Montes de León*. Which is yet another reminder to me of how pilgrimages are so important here.

The knights also restored Rabanal's tiny Iglesia de Santa Maria de la Asuncion in the thirteenth century. This *iglesia* sits directly across the street from the bench where I am now.

I'm looking at the church. It is small, primitive, made of sandstone. The church is attached to a Benedictine monastery, which is the only place open in town, save for a small café and one lone mercado that is about the size of a guest bathroom.

I fiddle for a few hours until the town is empty. All the pilgrims are gone. All the happy hikers are on the trail. I pack up my fiddle. I cross the desolate street with my case in hand. This is the third time I have visited the church, but each time I enter I definitely feel something. Something calming. And warm. The church's stone walls hold warmth, and I am able to shed my jacket.

The interior of Iglesia de Santa Maria is small, with ancient fresco colors painted on its twelfth-century stone arches. God himself only knows how old those paintings are. Older than my ancestors. Older than my ancestors' ancestors.

I sit in silence, feeling and looking at the frescos.

I decide to say a prayer. I have been praying a lot lately. Truthfully, I didn't expect to pray much while walking the Camino. But then, I didn't expect a lot of things. Looking back, I suppose what I thought the Camino would be was a really long, amazing, restorative, wonderful youth-group trip. I thought we'd see Spain at eye level, eat several *tortas* for breakfast, drink beer for lunch, wolf down heaps of carbs for supper, then fall asleep in our bunks. I thought we'd enjoy the company of pilgrims, share meaningful conversations, and deeply enrich the quality of our iPhone photo collection.

But it hasn't been this way at all.

The Camino is not a spiritual vacation. The Camino is not a reflective hike. The Camino is a living thing. The trail has its own personality and its own ideas. It is almost as if the Camino knows you're on it, feels your soles treading its dirt, and knows what it's going to do with you. For as long as you're connected to the Camino, in some way, it owns you. When you're out here, the Camino controls the elements of your daily life. What you will eat. Where you will sleep. Who you will meet, and why. What you will see, and whether it will have meaning. It knows whether you will suffer or rejoice.

Sean D.

The Camino sort of plans your education, without your consent. It ordains your catastrophes, orchestrates each lesson you must learn along the way, and chooses which dreams you will dream as you sleep. Everyone has wild dreams out here. I've had dreams. Important ones I still don't understand. My wife has had dreams. There really is something out here.

And the Camino does all this with the same seemingly impassive love a mother bluebird uses to nudge its babies from the nest. The Camino loves you. There is never any doubt about this. But that love, however, will sometimes hurt like a mother.

I pray in the church for nearly an hour. I am not sure what I'm praying for. I have given up praying for my legs. At this point, I am just praying I can adjust to whatever the Camino has planned for me.

I evidently fall asleep during my prayer, because I suddenly awaken in a slumped position, only to discover that I have been drooling on myself. It takes a moment to remember where I am. I half expect to be in my living room.

My eyes focus on the flickering candles that light the ancient domed room. And that's when I notice a symbol emblazoned on the altar candles. It is the same symbol on my rosary. I remove the rosary from my pocket and hold it up to the light. Definitely the same markings. I rise from my pew and approach the altar. I compare the symbols up close.

Interestingly, I've been seeing this symbol everywhere since we began the Camino. I haven't thought about this until now. But the symbol is everywhere. In small churches. Little nooks. It's not a symbol that is blatantly in your face like a crucifix, a Mary statue, or the Nike Corporation logo. Usually this symbol is tucked away, engraved upon something that is almost out of view.

I can't remember when exactly I started noticing this symbol on the Camino. But now I realize we see it all the time. Yesterday I caught myself drawing the symbol on a bar napkin. I even saw this symbol in one of my dreams last night. I realize all this sounds very woo-woo. And well, maybe it is.

After my prayer, I exit the chapel to find one of the monks

in his office. He is an older man. Cropped hair. Black robe. He is busy making bracelets using a magnifying glass.

I rap on his doorjamb.

"Excuse me," I ask. "May I ask you a question, sir?"

He tells me to come in. He speaks with a heavy German accent and says he is making these bracelets to help fund the monastery. So I purchase a bracelet, then I ask him about the symbol I saw earlier. I draw the symbol in the air.

He looks confused.

"I'm sorry," he says. "I do not follow."

"*This* symbol," I say. Then I air-draw it again, only bigger this time. "What does it mean?"

He smiles. "This is the Chi-Rho."

"What is the Chi-Rho?"

"It is ancient Greek. The very first Christians invented this symbol."

"Really?"

"The first-century followers would write this symbol, long before they were called Christians, back before it was a religion at all, back when people of different creeds and races would gather in secret, at someone's home, and share huge suppers. Gentiles and Jews, slaves and free men, peasants and magistrates. Back then, it was not a religion. It was just called The Way."

"So what does the symbol mean?"

"It means Christ. It means The Way."

Sean D

Libro Tres

I've been doing a lot of writing in this journal because everyone journals when they walk the Camino. All the tourist shops in the middle of little villages sell journals by the hundreds. Journals are almost as popular on this trail as shells. Also, I've been writing because I have plenty of time. It is our third night in Rabanal del Camino, and it seems like we've been here forever. Sean has been trying to heal, resting all day, keeping weight off his legs. But they aren't getting better. I am finally facing the fact that he might have to drop out. But we aren't talking about it.

When we walked into this tiny village on Saturday, Sean was badly limping, keeping pace several hundred feet behind me, struggling to keep up. No sooner had we entered Rabanal than we were immediately surrounded by angels. It has been such a beautiful experience, not lost upon us at all. The people here have shown us nothing but selfless love.

Tonight we just finished dinner downstairs in our hotel, where we met many other pilgrims. A young woman and her elderly dad, reconnecting by walking the Camino together. Our friend Frank from Australia. Two ladies from Bulgaria, in their seventies, old high school friends. We pilgrims in the dining room all knew each other. That's just how it is here.

Of course, our **main** topic over dinner was whether Sean feels up to walking tomorrow. He wants to try. But I really think he needs more rest. Still, if we don't start walking again soon, we won't make it to Santiago before we must fly home. We cannot live in Spain forever.

Sean doesn't know if his legs will make it. I have the same concerns, of course. If we keep walking tomorrow, it will not be easy. We will be crossing the León Mountains. The path will be rocky, with significant elevation gains and losses that murder even the strongest of legs.

Tomorrow is the Cruz de Ferro, the highest point on the Camino. Both literally and figuratively. This is the iron cross. The place we have all been waiting for. All the pilgrims are talking about it. Everyone has their rock. Sometimes they take the rock out and show it to you. Sometimes they explain what their rocks signify. Other times they just walk silently along, holding their rocks and praying. So tomorrow is a significant day for many pilgrims, and you can feel it in the air.

Sean and I haven't really discussed Plan B. It's just too painful to ponder. For the most part, Sean seems happy, but I can tell his spirit is falling. He's not sure what the following day will hold should he choose to hike again. And he doesn't want to be the reason we end our Camino. It's a hard choice, but before we go to bed, he tells me that he's gonna go for it. I pray his legs will hold.

We are walking again. *I* am walking again. But I shouldn't be. Each step feels like my shin is going to break. But I'm toughing it out the best I can. It is raining. We are up to our ankles in mud. We are crossing many creeks today, stepping on wobbly stones, which only makes my shins worse.

I am a quarter mile behind the math teacher. I can see her ahead. Now and then she waits for me to catch up, to make sure I am okay. But this is her Camino too. I keep telling her to keep walking at her own pace. Don't worry about me. I'm a big boy. I'll be fine. She walks ahead with the new friends we have met who are from Ukraine. I am bringing up the rear, wondering how I am going to complete another 250 kilometers of this trail.

The rain picks up tempo. Soon it is pouring. Rain is smacking on my cowboy hat so loudly I can hardly hear my own conscience. Pilgrims weave around me. I am leaning on a cane as I walk, doing anything to take a little extra weight off my shins.

Finally, the rain becomes torrential. Pilgrims are fast-walking around me on the trail, kicking up mud behind them as they sprint past. They are in a hurry because they are looking for shelter. Someone said there is a small church ahead; everyone is racing to look for it.

A few hundred meters away, I see a group of pilgrims huddled beneath a large tree to keep dry. The math teacher is in this group; she is waving at me to come and get out of the rain. But my eyes are drawn by something else.

In the middle distance stands a large iron cross.

WE'VE ALL BEEN TOLD ABOUT THE CROSS, OF COURSE. IT'S one of the most famous landmarks on the Camino. The *Cruz de Ferro*. The cross is located at the highest point of the Camino de Santiago. We are between Foncebadón and Manjarín, overlooking miles of farmland.

"It's taller than I thought," says the math teacher.

The rain is hammering even harder now. I am standing under the tree with the math teacher.

There are people standing at the cross, heedless of the downpour. We can see their silhouettes. Heads bowed. We can sense their reverence, even from this great distance. They are placing objects at the foot of the structure. Some objects are large, removed from their backpacks. Other objects are small enough to fit in their pockets.

The rain is slamming onto the earth. My palm leaf cowboy hat is dripping at the brim like a leaky gutter. My father's hat has been a godsend on the trail. You never realize how functional a cowboy hat truly is until you wear one in the rain.

I've been wearing a cowboy hat since I was a boy. My father wore cowboy hats, and he wore them non-ironically. I come from farmers and cattlemen. It's just what they did.

When the pilgrims leave the foot of the cross, I feel something pulling me to the monument. Almost like my feet are moving without my brain's permission. Maybe my brain knows that now is a good time to visit the cross since nobody else is making a move in this heavy rain. I leave the shelter of the trees and began walking toward the hill.

"Hey," my wife calls out. "You're going in the rain?"

"I'll only be a second."

"Why now?"

"Because I think it's my turn."

I HOBBLE TO THE CROSS. I AM WALKING CAREFULLY, STEPping around the mudholes and avoiding rocks. My shins are throbbing something fierce.

The cross rises from a mound of discarded pebbles that is

so large, you have to climb up it. When you view this thousand-year mound of stones up close, it will move you.

They come from all over the world. From history itself. Maybe even from your ancestors.

Many stones are decorated with artwork. Some are carved. Also, there are many objects that are not stones. Photographs wrapped in sandwich bags. Hair ribbons tied around wilting flowers. Crucifixes made of sticks. Notecards. Wedding rings. There are farewells to loved ones, written on looseleaf pages, covered in cursive, with ink bleeding in the rain. Baby shoes.

I reach into my pocket.

I have three rocks to place at the cross. I have been carrying them since Day One. It doesn't matter what these rocks represent. I am too proud to share the depths of my greatest pain. But it's a funny thing about carrying rocks. After staying in your pocket for so many weeks, they become like old friends. And even though they're heavy, even though they are uncomfortable, they're *your* rocks. You don't really want to let them go. You've been through a lot together.

But you must. You must let them go. So I do. I toss my pebbles at the foot of the cross. I spend maybe fifteen minutes there, just looking at them.

The rain begins to let up a little. Now it's just spitting. Pilgrims exit their shelter tree and begin the Camino again. My wife is waiting for me at the bottom of the hill. So I turn to walk away from the cross.

That's when I feel a voice.

I don't *hear* the voice. I sense it.

It is in my chest. Like the sound of your mom's voice when she's waking you up for school, and you're still caught between sleep world and reality world. Her voice is motherly, maternal, as she gently shakes you awake. "Wake up, sleepyhead." Her loving voice reverberates across both worlds and into your consciousness. Her words are fuzzy, but you know what she's saying. You know her motherly tone, and you feel her love as she gently wiggles you in your bed.

This is the kind of voice I feel. My whole life I've been told God is a man's man. And maybe he is. But what I need right now is a mom. And that's what I am given.

I stare at the mound of rocks.

"You have one more burden to leave," the voice says.

That's when I know the cross wants my hat.

This hat was my dad's. Sort of. I bought this hat when I visited his hometown decades ago. I visited his hometown for the sole purpose of forgiving him, so it was significant for me. It is maybe one of the most special things I own. I bought the hat in a desperate attempt to forgive my dad for decades of domestic abuse, for trying to kill my mother, for killing himself at the age of forty-two. For ruining our homelife with gun violence. For robbing me of who I was supposed to be and making me a sad person.

I remove my hat.

The hat is heavier than I remember. Faded from years of sunlight, rain, and sweat. This hat has traveled with me everywhere. Hiked every trail. Accompanied me on every road trip. I've worn this hat in almost every US state.

I weep.

But they aren't tears of sorrow. These are tears of another origin. I don't exactly know how to describe them. They are neither joyous, nor sorrowful. Neither are they angry tears, nor beautiful. They are bitter. Like gall in my mouth.

The voice is now telling me that this hat is my pain. This is the pain I carry. Every day. I carry this pain by choice. I wear it on my head, for all to see. This pain covers my scalp, and at times is the only thing standing between me and heaven.

I've been obsessed with my pain for years. I've been so preoccupied with it that it's made me almost narcissistic. I've let pain make me self-righteous and proud. I've let pain cause me to see myself as a perpetual victim. I've let pain replace optimism. I've let pain fester inside me and grow infected. I've let pain make me afraid. I've let pain make me half of a man. I've allowed my pain to make decisions for me. I have allowed pain to use me to hurt others.

I put the hat down.

I heave and cry. Until I can't see anymore. It is no longer raining. But I am. Finally, I stagger off the hill of stones.

Nearby pilgrims are asking if I am okay. My wife rushes to me. We embrace. She asks whether I'm okay.

I smile, wipe my face, and say, yeah, I am okay. And this time, maybe for the first time in my whole life, I mean it.

The mood was very somber as we walked. Sean wasn't his usual chatty self. He was in physical pain, I could tell. Although he seemed lighter, too, after visiting the Cruz de Ferro. I was still thinking about what I left behind at the cross. A burden I've been meaning to lay down for many years. A personal sorrow. One I'm not sure

I'm ready to share in this journal.

It was a gray day, drizzling off and on. Sean's head was soaking wet. His hair was matted to his forehead. Sometimes it rained heavily. Sometimes not.

We walked very slow for Sean's benefit. It was hard for me to walk so slow. I never realized how hard it is to walk slow.

But we are in this together, and I wanted to walk together. Especially today, after finally laying our rocks at the iron

cross.

We were only able to manage

ten miles. This means we are

falling behind schedule, and

quickly. We are not going to

finish if we keep coming up short

like this. But Sean can only do

what he can do. I can see he's

trying so hard.

We decided to stop in El

Acebo for the night. El Acebo is

very old, with stone streets,

stucco storefronts, and clay roof-

tops. It looks like your typical

quaint Spanish village. The albergue is at the edge of town, facing the Galician Mountains. The mountains look huge and green. Like rockier versions of the Appalachians. They are very pretty.

I have a knowing in my heart. I know, deep inside my-self, that Sean is not going to be able to walk any farther. I don't want to say this aloud. My family never talks about painful things aloud. We just ig-nore these things and hope they go away. But I am afraid if I say anything out loud, our trip will be over once I say the words. I know he doesn't want this trip to be over. I don't want this trip to be over either. It's been too wonderful to end now.

But when he got to the room, he collapsed on the bed and massaged his legs until he fell asleep. His legs were swollen and cartoonish. I left the room to find ice at the restaurant next door, but the Spanish are not big ice users. I had to visit a few different places to find any. When I returned with the ice, he was awake. He was sitting on the edge of the bed, staring into space. He looked at me with serious eyes and said, "I'm done."

We just held each other for a long time.

So our Camino is over, I was thinking. We are going home. But Sean said no. He said he wants me to keep walking without him.

There were tears in my eyes. There were tears in his eyes.

"Keep going?" I said. "You mean, without you?"

"This is your Camino, honey," he said. "Don't miss it."

Later, we went to supper with several other pilgrims. Sean limped down the street to the restaurant. I hated seeing him like this. He could hardly walk.

At supper, Sean sat across from me. We saw a precious young woman named Coline, whom we'd met earlier. She was struggling with blisters and a hurt ankle. Sean had helped dress her wounds this morning and we became fast friends. Coline and Sean have hatched a plan to catch a cab tomorrow, then they will take a series of buses to the next biggest city. Sean says he can take a cab to the next village and then meet up with me.

But this will mean I have to cross the Galician Mountains

alone. I have never done any-thing like this alone. I am afraid. But something inside me is telling me that I must do this. Something inside, a voice maybe, is telling me that I am supposed to do this.

He rested a hand on mine.

"You've got this," he said, "you're the strongest person I know."

But I am not strong. I've never been strong. I want to cry again. But this isn't the time or the place for crying.

Dinner was lively and fun. Sean played fiddle for everyone after dinner, and they all sang and cheered. When the pilgrims heard that Sean was quitting the trail, they hoisted him onto their shoulders and paraded him around the room. They said, "We will carry you to Santiago, Sean!" He was smiling and laughing, high upon their shoulders, but I could tell by the way he looked at me that he was hurting inside.

As they paraded him

around the restaurant, I was thinking about how these people, each from his or her own country, had never met me or Sean before the Camino, and yet they were promenading him around the room on their shoulders, proclaiming how much they loved us. I have never experienced friendship like this in my life.

But as I watched them carry my husband through the crowded restaurant, as I listened to all the pilgrims cheer, as I saw everyone smile at me, I felt an underlying melancholy. I knew this was the end of our Camino together. I knew that the Camino is like life. Sometimes you are fortunate enough to walk beside someone you love. Sometimes you walk alone.

Before I fell asleep, I held him tightly. He wiped the tears from my cheeks.

The last words he said before I fell asleep were:

"This is your Camino."

ORNING. MY WIFE AND I ARE IN THE LOBBY OF the albergue. She is crying into my chest. It's the kind of crying you do when you don't care who is watching. All the pilgrims are buzzing around us, paying no attention to the weeping woman. They are too busy getting ready for their day on the Camino. There's a big day ahead. There are mountains out there, and they aren't going to hike themselves.

White fog hangs over distant peaks and summits, hovering atop green mounts like Aladdin's carpet. The Galician Massif mountain range is like nothing I have ever seen. The mountains are jagged, but green and soft in some places. They are blocky and square, like big boulders that have been dropped from heaven into the soft earth below them.

I am holding my wife as she cries. Her head, tucked against my chest. Meanwhile, the lobby is alive with energy. Pilgrims are unpacking and repacking their backpacks, stuffing belongings into tiny drybags, then shoving these bags into slightly larger drybags, then, finally, cramming these big bags into even bigger backpacks. They lace and re-lace their boots three, four, five times, to get the right degree of tightness. They refill empty water bottles. They have a long way to go.

My wife and I stand at the door. Saying farewell. It will be

a few days before we see each other again. My taxi has just arrived. The driver looks at me. He is in no mood to wait.

"*Venga*," he barks. Which in this instance means, essentially, "Hurry up."

We are embracing. It is an immersive, full-body, American hug. You can say whatever negative thing you want about Americans, and you'd probably be right about us. But despite our political vitriol; despite our exploded sense of self-entitlement; despite our self-congratulatory demeanor; despite our classical ineptness within other countries, we are huggers. And that counts for something. When an American president gets sworn in, he hugs members of his cabinet. When an American baseball team wins a World Series, they hug in a big dog-pile. We Americans hug one another for every conceivable occasion, including the onset of daylight-saving time.

The math teacher and I rub one another's back. We press our hearts together, holding each other long and hard. I remember the first day I met her. The one thing I hated about that day was leaving her and going home. I never wanted to leave her. I didn't want to go home. She is my home.

We have walked three hundred and fifty miles together, through peaks and valleys. We have traversed river basins, miles of flowering canola fields. We have done our laundry in sinks in random albergues, laughing from drinking too much beer on empty stomachs. We have played solitaire on albergue bunks, amidst a world of sleeping pilgrims. We crossed the Pyrenees together. We have done everything together. We have always done everything together.

But my legs are unable to endure a moment more.

This magnificent brunette, whom I met on the Camino of My Own Life, before I was old enough to consume alcohol, is saying goodbye. The beautiful woman who wore a baby blue blouse on the night I knew I would marry her. The woman who imbued me with the audacity to be myself. This woman who not only helped me grow up, but grew up alongside me.

"I am afraid to do this trail without you," she says, wiping tears.

"Don't be."

"I don't want to be without you."

"That can never happen."

"I'm afraid I won't make any friends out there."

"You'll have to beat them away with a stick."

"What if I fall?"

"What if you don't?"

"What if I'm not strong enough?"

"What if you are?"

"What if I can't do it?"

"What if you thrive?"

The cabdriver is now growing impatient. He honks his horn. He taps his watch dramatically. My wife and I release each other and her face breaks wide open as I walk away.

"Goodbye," she says.

"It's only for a little while."

"I love you," she says.

"I love you more."

I can still taste her salty tears on my lips. I limp toward the minivan. I stow my backpack and fiddle case in the rear compartment. I feel a lump of clay in my throat. And my eyes are threatening to rain. But I want more than anything to impart any little bit of strength in me to my wife as I leave her. I want her to see me happy. I want her to see me smiling and joyful. Not full of sorrow. I nail a smile to my face.

"You've got this," I say.

She is covering her face with both hands, her shoulders heaving.

You cannot plan your own life. No matter how you toil and spin, no matter how you worry and fret, no matter how you organize and schedule, you cannot plan life. It just happens to you.

I step into the car. I close the vehicle door.

The driver looks at me in the mirror. He is not happy.

"I'm sorry," I say in Spanish.

He says nothing. He just throws the car into gear and off we go.

The passenger beside me is Coline, a Belgian lawyer. She's a very put-together woman whose blisters have paused her Camino experience. She is speaking Spanish with our cabdriver, telling him where we need to go. But I am staring out the window at the lovely brunette who is looking back at me. I am not really here. I'm out there with her in my heart.

The cab drives away.

I can see Jamie in the distance, her hand raised in farewell. She watches me fade into the Galician Mountains. Her silhouette grows smaller. So strong. So brave. So valiant, this woman. So brimming with life. So wholly and everlastingly blessed with the magically rare gift of smart-assity. This woman who stood beside a wayward and tragic boy at an altar, twenty-two years ago. A boy who was neither sure where he was going, nor how the hell he would get there. She was my Isolde, I her Tristan. She is Juliet, and I am Romeo. She is my Snow White, and I am the Seven Dwarves. Our names have always been said together. "Jamie and Sean." And always in this order.

I am sitting slumped in my seat, looking out tinted windows, watching the Galician Massif ranges rise and fall as the landscape swallows our cab whole. Impossibly verdant hills fly past us. The warm sun breaks through the fog and ushers in the pink sky of the morning. The fog disintegrates from the hilltops, then regathers again as quickly as it retreated. Then it begins to rain.

"Are you okay?" says Coline beside me.

"Yeah, I'm fine," I say.

Then she hands me a tissue.

When I first met Sean, I knew almost immediately that he would become my husband. Only two days after I met him, I remember telling one of my close friends that I was going to marry him. The words just popped out. As if I already knew they were true. I've heard it said that when you know you know.

I knew.

I hiked through the mountains of León, through the cold of morning, clutching my backpack straps, and I remembered the first night Sean and I spent time together. We didn't want to leave one another's company—we stood in a parking lot and talked until around one in the morning, only parting when it started to rain. After that night, we spent all of our free time to-gether. Every single day. We just wanted to be together. Once we were married, whole years went by that we didn't spend one night apart.

Repacking my backpack each morning has been a major ordeal. You would think after many days on the trail, I'd be able to pack in record time, but that isn't the case. It takes forever. Once the bag is full, I have to attach leftover items to the backpack with carabiner clips. That's how much stuff you carry out there. Objects swing from your pack all day as you walk. With each step, you can hear stuff clinking against your scallop seashell.

The scallop shell is on everyone's backpack out here. The shell is an important part of the Camino, the most noticeable icon on the trail. It's on every trail marker, painted on walls and street corners, printed on terracotta tiles, embedded in pavement, mounted to posts, and carved on trees.

Sean and I received our ceremonial shells when we both

registered at the pilgrims' office in Saint-Jean-Pied-de-Port. We each chose a single scallop shell to attach to our backpack. Attaching a shell to your pack is a big deal. It shows that you are out here for a reason. It shows that you're serious. Some pilgrims bring special shells with them from home. Others carry shells with loved one's names painted on them.

This morning my backpack was on the bed, half packed. I was getting ready when I noticed something lying next to my backpack. Sean's shell.

With trembling hands and tears in my eyes, I used a length of string to secure his scallop shell to my backpack, next to my own.

Saying goodbye was hard. There were lots of tears, lots of long hugs that neither of us wanted to end. Finally his taxi disappeared, and I was all alone. I am heartbroken for him. And for me. And for us.

The mountains were muddy

this morning. I was trying to step carefully, alone on the trail, as fog rose from the treetops. It was such an isolating feeling being by myself. Eerie, almost. As I walked, I was thinking about how Sean didn't let me see his disappointment when I left him. Instead, he encouraged me and told me that he is proud of me. He says I am going to finish strong.

Although I am alone on this trail, and heartbroken, the truth is, I want to keep doing this. I want to walk the Camino. I can't explain why.

My parents didn't travel. My father never had time for travel. All he did was work. All he did was take care of his family. My mother would have enjoyed seeing more in her life too, but never did. She never admitted that she wanted to. She resigned herself to the life she had. She never went anywhere. Never saw anything. She lived in a small town, lived in a small world, and never even tasted pizza until her mid-fifties.

Maybe her life was half lived. I don't know. Maybe she would have done the Camino if only she'd had the chance. So I am carrying my mother in my heart all these miles. I tell myself that I'm walking for her. I don't want my life to be half lived.

—

The terrain was tricky. The descent from El Acebo was very steep and the ground was rocky.

The views of the Montes de León with the low-hanging clouds were beautiful today. I was alone all morning. I would've texted Sean, but my phone had no service.

I stopped in Molinaseca for an early lunch. It's a charming town. I ate a huge sandwich. I am eating my feelings today. While I sat, two American ladies stopped to chat. Sean and I met them several days earlier.

It was comforting to see familiar faces, even if I couldn't

recall their names.

Back to the trail. I climbed hills and weaved along a steep path. When I got close to Ponferrada, which is a bigger city, I could hardly believe I'd come this far on my own.

I was a few miles from Ponferrada when I made new friends on the trail. Their names are Iryna and Viktoriia, two twenty-two-year-olds from Ukraine. They are best friends who wear matching purple jackets

and pants, and even purple
shoes. They look like the Bobbsey
Twins. I call them the "Purple
Girls." I cannot express how
happy I am to meet the Purple
Girls. What a breath of fresh air
they are. Like purple salve for

my broken heart.

The Purple Girls had been joined by Henry, a twenty-year-old college student from Texas, who is mostly silent but friendly. They all call me "JJ," just like my nieces do. Which makes me feel old. Still, I love being called "JJ." It makes me feel like I have family out here.

Even though the Purple Girls were young and fit, they acted like walking over ten miles a day was going to put them in an early grave. I convinced them to keep walking with me all the way to Camponaraya for the night, which was close to sixteen miles. They hesitatingly agreed to join me, but they were grumbling the whole way like kids do. So I told them to suck it up—I used to teach high-school algebra.

When I arrived, I was tired. It was quiet in my room. I realized I was really out here by myself now. I lifted up my phone to text Sean. Message cannot be sent, the phone said. I wanted to throw my phone against a wall.

I ended up having dinner with friends Sean and I had met last night and am so grateful for their company. I no **longer** felt quite so lonely. I ate some of the best food I have tasted. Then again, maybe it just tasted that way because of all I have been through.

Tonight is the first night that Sean and I are apart.

MY TAXI ARRIVES AT VILLAFRANCA DEL BIERZO AFter a long, twisty, pleasant ride through the mountains. And by "pleasant" I mean that only one of three taxi passengers actually vomited. I paid our driver, then found a nearby bush where I could double over and join the fun.

I part ways with Coline, saying goodbye in French. She wishes me well, hugs me, and requests that I never speak French again. I limp along cobbled streets toward my bus stop, leaning on a cane. A young woman pilgrim joins me. We are both lame pilgrims. Her name is Marie and she is from Virginia. And when she learns I am American, we both get excited. Namely, because English is at a premium out here. Moreover, nobody can properly mutilate English like we from the Southern United States.

I ask what is wrong with my new friend's leg. At first she doesn't answer, she just looks like she is going to cry.

"I think I have a sprained ankle," she says.

Marie is nineteen. This is the first time she has ever been away from home. Her mother did not want her to do this trail. She called it "foolish" and a "waste of money." But Marie came out here anyway. She says she is here to find guidance in her life, and clarity. She needs clarity now more than ever, she says, because her father died two years ago from pancreatic cancer. Marie and her mother were his primary caregivers.

A seventeen-year-old should not have to watch her father die, she says. She says she has felt lost ever since his funeral. Marie hooks arms with me for stability. Together we limp through the streets of Villafranca.

We find a bar-slash-café where we can get out of the rain and wait for our bus. We sit at the bar. The bartender hands us menus. We order two *cafés*. The coffee is pleasantly hot and utterly destroys the skin on the roof off my mouth. Just the way I like it.

I text Jamie several times, but our phone service isn't co-operating today. None of my messages go through. There are error messages telling me to try again. I finally put my phone away and gaze out the window. I know she's out there, in those mountains, alone. I can feel her.

Marie seems kind of drawn to me. I can tell. This is likely because I am about her father's age. I know what she is feeling. Sometimes you just want to be around someone who reminds you of your dad. Someone older than you who either knows what the hell he's doing, or fakes it really well.

We have hours to kill, and I am grateful to be sitting at this bar, off my shin-splinted legs, which are throbbing like the bass track to a top-forty disco hit. The café is warm. Talk radio is playing overhead. And although the radio voices speak too rapidly in *Español* for me to understand, I can tell by the ad-renal, hateful tones that we are listening to the international language of politics.

Marie and I sit on stools and watch the mirror behind the bar, which displays a room full of locals consuming their morning beers along with ample handfuls of cigarettes. In the mirror, I can see that Marie is downcast. She isn't texting any-one on her phone; she isn't taking pictures of her coffee like other young pilgrims would. She isn't doing anything but sit-ting here, staring.

"You gonna be okay?" I ask.

"I don't know."

I look at Marie's lower leg, which is taped. Just like mine.

"Does it hurt?" I ask.

"Everything hurts."

"I'll drink to that."

We toast coffees.

The bartender checks on us again. She is older. Tall and slender, with bottle-blonde hair. She moves behind the bar with the ease of someone who's been doing this awhile.

She looks at my nineteen-year-old friend and says something in Spanish. Young Marie looks at me, waiting for translation. But I didn't quite understand. The bartender snaps at Marie again in Spanish. This time I think I see tears gathering in Marie's eyes. She is nineteen and lost in a foreign country.

"I don't know what she's saying to me," says Marie.

"She wants to know if you want anything to eat," I say.

I can see the girl calculating the prices on the menu in her head. Mental math is hard when you don't think in euros.

"Can you tell her I'll pass?" Marie says.

So I speak to the bartender in Spanish, but I do not translate Marie's exact words—per se. The bartender brings food and sets it before me. I nudge the plate toward Marie and ask for her assistance consuming the oversized chocolate croissant. Politely she declines. But in the end, I win. Because, as I said, it is a chocolate croissant.

"What was your dad's name?" I ask.

There is already chocolate smeared on Marie's chin. "His name?"

"*Sí.*"

She just looks at the croissant longingly.

I lost a parent at a young age too. Everyone always tells you they're sorry when you lose someone. But nobody ever asks their name. Sometimes you go years without saying the name. Sometimes it feels so nice just to say their name.

"Andrew," she says.

"Nice name."

"What do you think I should do?" she finally asks. "Should I keep walking the Camino, or go back home? I don't think my ankle can take any more of this abuse."

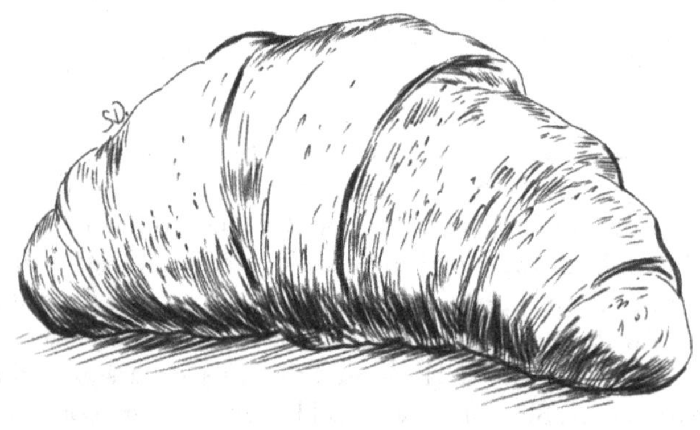

But I have no advice. Because the hard truth is, I am in the same boat.

"I wish I had my dad to ask," she says.

"Me too," I say.

She picks at the croissant.

We sit in silence for a while.

Finally, a few Americans join us for a spell. They are pilgrims she has evidently met on the trail before. They are loud and fun, students from the University of Wisconsin with sunny dispositions and great senses of humor. But Marie barely says three words. She remains a spectator.

When the Americans leave us, Marie says, "I feel so confused."

I nod.

I've spent my whole life confused.

"Just tell me what should I do," says Marie. "I need some advice."

But it's a trap. She is waiting for me to do what all middle-aged American guys do when posed with an existentialist question: pretend we have the answer. Even though the sad honesty is—the eternal truth we men are so afraid to admit—we are full of bovine ordure.

"I can't tell you what to do," I tell her. "I'm right here with you. I don't know what I'm doing out here. I don't know where I'm going. I don't know what I should do either."

Marie grows silent for a while. The croissant is decimated. And I'm assuming it was delicious because this pastry did not live long enough for me to sample.

"What are you afraid of?" she asks me.

"I don't know. I think I'm afraid of missing the Camino."

She is silent for a long time.

"Me too," she finally says.

The bartender brings another chocolate croissant. Marie digs in before I even reach my fork.

"But you know," she says, dabbing chocolate from her face, "it's pretty stupid to be worried about missing the Camino when you think about it. I mean, we're *on* the Camino, whether we physically walk the path or not. *This* is the Camino. *Life* is the Camino. Right?"

She takes another bite.

Marie is experiencing a definite sugar high.

"And you know what else?" she says, pointing her fork at me. "I think the awareness we've cultivated out here is making me realize that the Camino is not a trail at all. The Camino is wherever God is, right? Because God isn't just a place or a trail. The Camino is *here*. The Camino is *now*. It's everywhere. It's everything we see and do, everyone we meet. It's the journey. It's you. It's me. The Camino is life. That's the true Camino."

Your little girl is going to be just fine, Andrew.

The mountains seemed taller to-day. But I was **feeling** strong. I slept okay **last** night and woke up ready to hike.

I stopped for coffee and breakfast at a small café before leaving for the trail. At the café, the Purple Girls and Henry were already having breakfast. They said they wanted to walk with me to-day, but oddly, I told them I wanted to walk alone for a while. I don't even know why I said that. But something inside me wanted to walk alone.

I told them to go ahead without me. Before they left, Viktoriia gave me a bracelet she made of tiny beads, with the colors of the Ukrainian flag. Then she hugged me.

I was moved. I put it on. If this bracelet had been made of

gold and diamonds it could not have meant more.

I walked alone. Mud splattering. Rain falling. The mountains were incredible. I was getting closer to accepting the fact that, perhaps, walking without Sean is where my Camino actually begins.

I had a lot of time to think, and I came to the realization that I have used Sean as my social crutch for a long time. I let Sean be the outgoing one, the chatty one, the never-meet-a-stranger guy. As an extension of him, I get to meet all of these cool people too, but without taking any risk. But what is the risk? I ask myself.

What am I afraid of?

So I have decided that for my Camino, I am going to take this opportunity to force myself out of my comfort zone. I am going to meet people and be more proactive in starting conversations. I'm going to be more like the seventeen-year-old Jamie who was fearless and quirky and made no apologies for who she was.

The trail led deeper into the mountains. My legs were covered in sludge. My hair was wet with rain and perspiration. I smelled really bad. The sound of my feet was sort of hypnotizing.

Up ahead, I saw a purple blur in the distance. It was Iryna, Viktoriia, and Henry. They also had a new friend walking with them. A boy I didn't recognize.

I called out their names.

"Iryna! Viktoriia! Henry!"

"JJ!" they all shouted back.

It was a big reunion with lots of hugs and laughter.

"We thought you wanted to walk alone today," they said.

"I changed my mind," I said.

—

I walked with the Purple Girls and Henry and their new friend, Evan all day. We shared chocolate and cookies and candy and anything else that will make you fat. After a half day of walking, we came upon a village that looked practically deserted. We were looking for a place to eat but couldn't find anything. Many villages on the Camino seem almost like third-world places. Some of them are like ghost towns.

The Purple Girls and I were hungry; the cookies and chocolate weren't cutting it. As we walked onward, we were all fantasizing about what we would do if there was a McDonald's around the bend.

The Purple Girls said they would tear up a hamburger right now. I told them I would order a fish sandwich and bathe my underarms in tartar sauce.

Evan was silent at this remark.

I thought maybe he was trying to visualize tartar sauce dripping from my armpits. Then he finally told us that he is from Guernsey, an island off the coast of England. He said there are no fast-food restaurants in Guernsey. He had never even seen a McDonald's before.

"Wait!" said Iryna. "You've never had a chicken nugget?"

Evan shook his head.

"Do you even know what a Big Mac is?" asked Viktoriia.

The young man shook his head again.

"A big what?" he said.

"A Big Mac!" the Purple Girls shouted.

Evan kept shaking his head.

"A Big Mac, no. Come to think of it, I've never had a little one either. What is a Big Mac?"

The Purple Girls laughed and told Evan he was **much** better off for not knowing about them and he would probably live until a hundred and three and be skinny for the rest of his life. But I told him not to worry, he'll get fat someday like normal middle-aged people. Then we ate more chocolate.

MY TAXI DRIVER DOES NOT LIKE AMERICANS. I know this because of the way he spits the word *Americano* from his mouth, as though I am responsible for setting international policy. He charges Americans three times more than he charges people from other countries. I figured this out yesterday when I took this same taxi with a French woman who split the cab fare with me. The driver assumed I was French because of my companion passenger, so he charged me fifteen euros. This morning, however, when I tell the driver I am from Alabama, his demeanor changes. He scowls at me. He drives me less than a few miles and charges me fifty-five euros. When I pay fifty-five euros, I smile at him and say in Spanish, "This is a little expensive, no?"

"This is *my* tariff, *Americano*." Then he yanks the cash from my hand.

The driver seems surprised when I hand him an additional €10 tip.

I say in Spanish, "You deserve even more than this. You work very hard, sir."

He blushes.

Then he shakes my hand. But he doesn't squeeze very hard.

When he drives away, I am left standing in a nanoscopic

town, nestled snugly within the Galician Mountains. The rock-paved streets, the ancient buildings, and the crowing roosters are almost so perfect they look false. Like a movie set.

It has been raining for three days, and it's not letting up. I wander down the street toward my hotel.

It's Mother's Day back in the US right now. This morning at my hotel, I greeted a female hotel employee by wishing her a happy Mother's Day, whereupon she informed me that this was not Mother's Day in Spain, and that I would *know* when it was Mother's Day in Spain because it was a massive celebration with much food and dancing and wine and brass bands and fancy dresses and family coming back home and the whole country would pretty much shut down. She asked what Mother's Day was like in the US. I told her that Mother's Day in the US is a major event wherein American mothers are given the enormous honor of receiving a Hallmark card, and perhaps even a gift certificate to Outback.

I arrive at my hotel. The sign on the window says they will not be opening for another five hours. This place is so small there are evidently no restaurants open, no cafés open, no bars with their doors open. So I am compelled to sit outside like a beggar, waiting. In the rain.

The rain picks up, and I am sopping wet. From head to heel. Even so, somehow I'm in a great mood today. I did not expect to be in a good mood after the math teacher and I parted ways. I thought I'd be miserable. But something shifted inside me. It's simple, really: Because I am no longer walking the Camino, I do not *have* to walk the Camino. So the pressure is off. My personal Camino is, for the most part, finished. My work is done.

I now have the distinct pleasure of bumming around Spain without a schedule. Which I have been doing. I have been visiting every establishment that serves *tápas* and drinking Spanish beers like they need the bottles back. The locals seem to like me too. Which I can hardly believe. Most days I'm not even sure whether *I* like me. But the people here—with the exception of my cabdriver—are friendly, and very interested in the fiddle I carry.

And so I have been playing American fiddle tunes in tavern upon tavern where *Inglés* is seldom spoken. I limp into the bar and within a few seconds someone is asking me to play the instrument and offering me food. And I have learned a very important truth about mankind throughout this entire process, something I never knew before. I have learned that, in Spain, if you have shin splints, they give you free beer.

I spent yesterday in one such dimly lit stone tavern. The locals were mostly elderly people. They gathered around me, dressed in their woolen and cotton clothes, the old men wearing flatcaps, the old women wearing dresses. They asked me to play something. I told them, no, no, you don't want me to play. But then they started begging. Then one old man behind the bar clasped his hands together and pleaded. So I removed the fiddle from its case. I played "Martha Campbell" and "Money Musk." Two older Galicians hooked arms and began dancing until they almost fell over. And one elderly woman performed an aggressive solo dance that was more like stomping than dancing.

I am beginning to realize how important dancing is to the Spanish.

After I finished playing my fiddle in the tavern, everyone from *that* tavern marched me down the street to *another* tavern, en masse, where I played for a totally different saloon crowd of elderly people, this time drinking totally different beers. I felt I had died and woken up in a Hemingway novel.

The next tavern was rowdier than the first. Almost everyone in the room, both young and old, began to dance to the fiddle. One old man, who did not speak English, told me his father used to play the fiddle, and his father would often play for street dances. When the old man was a little boy, he said he would dance while his father played.

Then the old man showed me exactly how he would dance. His dance was proud and ancient, like a bullfighter. There was nothing unserious about his performance. He was dignified and tall, as if reaching out to me from another era. Then he taught me how to do it—or tried. He taught me how to hold my stomach, how to keep my spine board-straight. How to stamp my heels arrogantly and twirl, while keeping one hand suspended delicately above my head. The people in the bar laughed and hollered.

And now I sit outside my hotel. Still glowing from the past days.

My fiddle case is beside me, wrapped in a trash bag to protect it from the rain. But the rain is getting worse. Across the street I see a stone church. The doors are splayed open—I hadn't noticed them before—and a light is on. I sling my backpack over my shoulder and head across the muddy street, squishing in my boots, wincing in pain with each step beneath the weight, leaning on my cane.

I enter the church. I am dripping all over. I am cold. The stone walls chill the air. I can see my breath. I use a bandana to dry my wet body, but it's not working. Then I plop my dripping derrière onto a pew. The rain on the church roof sounds like white noise.

I still have five hours until the hotel opens. I check my phone. It has been a day since I've heard from the math teacher. Sometimes our phones work well in Spain. Most

times, however, Verizon sucks. Texting has become a luxury in this country.

I sit quietly in a pew, gazing at the ornate altar. And I have just realized that today marks the month anniversary of when we started the Camino. It seems like fifty years ago that we began walking. But it's only been thirty days. And within those thirty days, I can honestly say one of the most important things I have learned is: Nothing happens the way you want it to. Not in life. Not on the Camino. But in the end, I'm glad things don't always happen the way I want them to.

Or else maybe I never would've learned to dance.

I have a long walk ahead of me today. I set out early, just after sunrise. When my feet hit the trail, muscle memory kicked in, and I started walking without even thinking about it. I was walking with the Purple Girls in the kind of amiable silence that accompanies the Camino. You go through long bouts of quiet, then someone speaks. Then there will be a short burst of conversation, then it will die. Then it starts again. This is not at all like normal life, where you have to keep conversations going without any dead air.

Today is Mother's Day in the US. I am not a mother. But being out here alone, for all these days, walking with some of the young people, who all seem to glue themselves to me, I am wondering why they choose to be around me.

Maybe they sense the high school teacher in me. Maybe I am more maternal than I thought.

Anyway, I have been thinking a lot about motherhood. This is my fourth Mother's Day without my own mother. I guess I have nothing to celebrate. I am an orphan now since both my parents are gone. I spent the whole walk today thinking about my mother. "Mother Mary" is what we called her.

We were friends. Best friends. She was my world. And I was

hers. And it feels good to be someone's whole world.

I miss that feeling.

My mother used to keep a black-and-white composition notebook next to the chair where she always sat. The chair where she passed the majority of her daylight hours. I would write all the details of our work and travel schedule in this book. What city we were going to, how many nights we would be gone, which hotels we were staying in, what we were traveling for, what theater Sean would be performing in. And she would pull this notebook out several times each day and study where I was at that particular moment.

I have no doubt that she would be keeping up with me now too, if she were still alive. If she were alive right now, I know what would happen. One of her caregivers would bring out a map of Spain, unfold it until it took up the whole room. Then they'd use a highlighter to out-

line our route. Mother would

check our progress on Sean's blog.

She would know more about the

Camino than we would.

Part of me wonders what

she would think of us doing an

adventure such as this. Would she

have thought it was crazy?

Would she have ever desired to

do something like this when she

was younger, healthier? Did she

have the same sense of adventure

I have? Or did she keep this

desire hidden because she was a

mother and a wife, from a different and more buttoned-up era, and it was safer not to want things than it was to have dreams that only led to disappointment? Was she a world explorer in her fantasies?

I miss her so much. I miss seeing her out there in her garden, hands covered in soil, wearing her big floppy hat. I miss how slow she ate. I miss her dry sense of humor.

I take mental photographs in my brain and share them with

her in my imagination. Because I know she would love seeing these photos if she were still alive. I know she would love seeing Sean and me together. She would devour every detail I shared with her. She would smile every time we told her a story. She would have something funny to say. She would be the first to tell me how happy she was for me. Sometimes I think I feel her out here on the Camino. I'm sure it's just my imagination.

Iryna and I naturally paired

off and walked together while
Viktoriia and Henry walked
ahead. I asked Iryna why she
was walking the Camino.

Iryna's face seemed pained
at the question. She is such a
beautiful girl, with milk skin and
a brunette ponytail. Her eyes
were bright, and her cheeks were
rosy from the cold.

Iryna told me about her life.
Her family was an untraditional
one. She said her father took a
job in the US as a contractor
when she was very young. He

would be gone all year, except for returning to Ukraine once per year, for only a month. This was all she ever saw of him. They lived separate lives.

"So it was my mother who raised me," Iryna said. "My mother gave everything for me. And I mean **everything**."

Her mother's dream had been to live in the US with her father, but this had never been possible. Not until Russia invaded Ukraine. At this point, the US eased its borders and began allowing more Ukrainians to enter the country. Her father was overjoyed at the idea of finally bringing his family to the US. They would finally be a family again.

But Iryna was a high schooler at the time. She did not want to leave Ukraine. Her whole life was there. She had cousins and aunts and uncles and friends. But Iryna is an only child. If she had chosen to stay behind, Iryna would've been responsible for breaking up the family a second time.

"My mother has sacrificed so much for me."

So Ioryna came to the US with her mom. It was a brutal transition for such a young girl. She could hardly speak English when she first came to the US. A few years later, Ioryna was granted her green card. Which meant she could travel again, but this only made her future decisions harder.

"I am a young woman torn between countries," she said. "I

have so many friends in the US, but other than my parents, all my family is back in Ukraine."

There were tears in her eyes as she spoke. Hers is a soul divided between the old country and a new one. As a result, she has no idea what to do with her life. Where to live. Where to go to school. What to become. Who she really is.

And I realized, as she was speaking, that she was talking to me in the same way you would talk to your mother. I hooked arms with Loyna. I told her I wished I had some advice to give, but I didn't. When I was her age, I was partying like Janis Joplin. I didn't have a care in the world. I did not have to make life-altering decisions like this. But I told her not to worry. Life has a way of giving perspective, if you just give it time, I said. And I'm finding out that if you let it, the Camino has a way of showing you who you really are.

As these words exited my

mouth, I wondered if I was saying them to Iryna. Or if my mother was saying them to me.

—

It's a new day. There is so much green this morning. All around. Green rolling hills. Green mountains. Green cattle pastures. So many beautiful, doe-eyed cows. I talked to them all. I told them how beautiful they were. I told them all that I loved them. Today, I will be climbing **2,300** feet. But I have motivation. I am meeting Sean in O Cebreiro. But only briefly. He will **take** a bus to Sarria because the bus only runs once per day. I cannot wait to see him.

I miss him, but I am starting to feel better about what I'm doing. Not necessarily stronger, but a little more confident.

It was misting this morning. But that was better than snow. It snowed yesterday in some nearby villages. The weather here

is insanely unpredictable. Sometimes you get all four seasons in
one day.

Today's path was steep and
muddy. In some sections of
trail, I sank in the thick mud up
to my ankles. At other times, I
slid and almost fell.

I've learned that it helps to
look down at my feet when
walking up a steep hill. When I
take my eyes off my feet, I'm
reminded of the daunting ascent
ahead. But if I just take it one
step at a time, I'm good. This is

true in life, too.

I checked the time. I was a few hours behind schedule. The mud was really slowing me down. So I texted Sean to let him know that I was running late. But the text didn't go through. Message cannot be sent. Thanks, Verizon.

I hope like hell I'm losing weight out here. In one of the albergues, I once heard a lady say that only male pilgrims lose weight on the Camino, but women never do. She had a theory. She said most women have to work much harder than the average man to achieve these great distances. To do this, women have to eat more croissants than men.

The trail led to the village of La Faba. I emerged from the thicket covered in mud and grime. My hair was a mess. My clothes were drenched with rain.

I was looking at all the people gathered outside the village's only pub, I smelled coffee, and

the scent of baking bread. Everyone was eating lunch.

I decided it was time for a
croissant.

I AM STANDING AT A BUS STOP IN THE RAIN. ALThough to call this a "bus stop" is generous. It's just a highway guardrail.
I am alone on this empty highway, waiting to catch a ride out of O Cebreiro. I was supposed to meet my wife here, but I guess things didn't work out. Our phones aren't working, and I don't know where she is. I look into the distant mountains, and I know she's out there somewhere. But this is all I know. And besides, the bus is on a tight schedule. If I don't leave now, I won't be able to meet her in Sarria.

I haven't seen her for a long time now. We haven't had much phone contact because our phone service in this country is majestically crappy. I'm sure the math teacher is doing great, but I miss her.

The rain starts coming down heavily. There are hurricane-like winds kicking up, whooshing through O Cebreiro. I am nearly knocked off my feet. And just when things couldn't get any worse, someone starts playing bagpipes. There is a guy standing beneath an archway, playing bagpipes at full volume. The droning tones reverberate throughout the mountains and through the streets of O Cebreiro.

O Cebreiro is a tiny, prehistoric village, entirely made of stone and thatch, with a Pigeon Forge vibe. The tourist gift shops and tourist-trap pubs operate a thriving trade, selling pilgrim essentials like trinkets, walking sticks, handkerchiefs, seashells, and probably even monogrammed toilet paper. Still, it is the most majestic village I think I've ever seen in my life. The mountains in the distance are brilliant green, rising like swells in an ocean of fog. These are not the beer-commercial Rockies, nor the ski-brochure Alps. These are distinctly Spanish mountains. There is a strong Celtic history in this region of Spain. They had bagpipes here long before the Irish did.

I should be angry or bitter about the rain. I should be jealous that my wife is somewhere out there, hiking deep within those mountains as I limp through Spain on shin-splinted calves. But I'm maybe happier than I've been in a long time, slumming around the Iberian Peninsula with nowhere to be, no schedule to follow, and no one to please but my bartenders. Bartenders who keep giving me free beer until either I quit playing the fiddle or I fall off my stool. Whichever comes first.

Also, I've met throngs of injured pilgrims, just like me, who are unable to walk the trail anymore. They have battered knees, bloody feet, or shin splints worse than mine. There are scores of these wounded pilgrims scattered along the periphery of the trail, sitting in each café, riding in each bus or train, limping through each village, trying to salvage their Camino experience the best they can.

Which is why yesterday I decided that I am going to assume a different role on the Camino. No longer will I be the troubadouring fiddler who breezes through town and drinks everyone's beer. I will now be a medic who breezes through town and drinks everyone's beer.

So I stocked up on bandages at the local pharmacy. I carry them in my backpack. I have been handling a lot of sweaty feet lately. I've been treating blisters all along the trail, wrapping the infected sores of fellow pilgrims, helping however I can. If this is my calling on the Camino, to be an amateur foot medic, I'm okay with that. Some French lady nicknamed me "*le medic pathetique.*"

I check my watch. The bus is supposed to be here by now. The bus runs once per day in O Cebreiro, at 3:22 p.m., which in global time is 15:22, or perhaps it's 16:22, or maybe

it's 538:31:29. There's no way for me to know for sure because I'm American. I don't think in global time.

After standing in the rain for a few hours, my spirits are
starting to fall. I am hungry. My stomach is churning, and I
am getting cold. I still have a lot of transit ahead of me, and
the day is mostly over. I can't quit shivering. I just want to be
somewhere warm.

That's when I notice a female pilgrim coming off the trail.
I notice her gait first. A confident stride, with a little "wanna
party?" thrown in. A bouncy walk. I know this woman.

I see other pilgrims walking alongside her as she makes
her journey toward me. They are young pilgrims. They are
healthy. And two of them are very purple. These pilgrims all
clap her shoulders and laugh in unison with her. It looks like
this woman is their troop leader. A few days on the trail, and
the math teacher is already someone's leader.

I smile.

Seeing her, there in the distance, I no longer feel cold. I
am no longer quivering. The woman eventually sees me
standing at the bus stop. Her face changes. She starts jogging
when she sees me. She careens into me. She throws her arms
around my neck. And I feel grateful.

"Hey," I say.

"Hey."

"How are you?"

She is drenched. Breathless. And flush.

"I'm great! How are you?"

She is covered in mud, and her hair is sopping wet.

"Proud," I say.

"Of what?"

"Of whom."

We talk some. We take a selfie. But our time is short. She
needs to keep moving. She has a lot of trail left, and daylight
is disappearing. And I have a bus to catch. I watch the lovely
woman walk away, shrinking into the distance, finally vanish-
ing on the trail with nothing but herself, her friends, and my
love.

The sun is getting lower. I have been walking all day. I need to get off my feet. The trail is darker than I expected, the trees draped over the trail like thick curtains. I am still going uphill. Surely it's going to be downhill at some point, right? I mean, isn't that how mountains work?

The mist is getting heavier, it's raining, it's windy and it's forty-four degrees. The trail is darkening as the sun lowers itself behind the mountains.

I check my phone. No service. Verizon can kiss my you-know-what.

The hills are relentless today. I finish one uphill and am met with an even steeper one after that. I don't know if I can do this anymore. I don't know if I want to do this anymore. I am losing my resolve.

What I need is encouragement. What I need is company. What I need is more croissants.

But I am alone. I hike upward until the narrow, tree-lined path opens up a little. I can see mountains beyond, against the darkening sky. The intensity of wind and rain immediately picks up. I wish I wasn't here right now. The wind is so cold and strong that my face stings. My hat keeps blowing off, and I can't hear anything because the wind is so loud.

In the distance I see something. At first, I think it's a

fellow pilgrim, so I wave. But as I get closer, I can see that it's not a person. It's a giant statue of a pilgrim.

The statue at **Alto de San Roque** depicts an ancient pilgrim. His sandaled feet are covered with Band-aids from all the pilgrims who pass this statue and place a bandage on his ankles and feet. The pilgrim is holding his hat down on his head, turning his face from the wind. He is alone.

I approach the monument and

touch his ruined feet. I tell him I know how he feels. I am breathless. I am in awe. I am in tears.

I stand here for a long time, just looking at him. I cannot describe how comforting it is seeing him, knowing what his ancestors went through. Knowing what pilgrims throughout the ages have gone through. They went through this. Exactly what I am going through now.

This statue reminds me that, although I am walking by myself, I am not alone. Millions have gone before me. Their burdens, heavier than mine. Their feet, worse off than my own. I kiss the tips of my fingers and touch my fingers to his tired feet. And I keep walking.

—

It's evening. All pilgrims have already stopped for the day. And I am still hiking. The pilgrims are all in their rooms, lying in their bunks, showered and clean, scrolling phones, FaceTiming with loved ones. While I am walking in the rain.

I am raw and emotional. My legs no longer hurt; they are just numb. My feet feel like heavy basketballs. The mud from the trail clings to the soles of my shoes, making them weighty. My hands are frozen. My face hurts from the biting gale.

This is one of the hardest days I have had on the trail. Maybe one of the hardest days I've had in my life. Both physically and mentally. Thankfully, I finally have phone service atop the mountain. I am texting with friends, my sister, my sister-in-law, and of course, Sean. Their encouragement means more than they will ever know. At one point, I text Sean, through tears, that I want to call a cab, but this is impossible. I am in the middle of nowhere. Like, "mountainous nowhere." Like, the most "nowhere" I've ever seen. That kind of "nowhere."

As the hours drone on, I am beyond lonely. I am melancholy, and worst of all, I've eaten all my chocolate. Right now, I wish I could call Sean for company, for encouragement, for a big ol' pep talk. But my phone battery is getting low, so I have to quit texting to save it for emergencies only.

Time is moving so slow. The miles are moving even slower. I want to sit down and cry. I want to stop walking and lie down beneath a tree and go to sleep.

But I must put one foot in front of the other and keep walking. This is my Camino. This is all part of a bigger plan. Maybe I'm here because I need to see, I need to learn, I need to believe in something. Believe that I can. Believe that I am not alone, even when I am.

I finally arrive at my albergue. I am cold. I am damp. I am hungry. I am almost debilitated. But I did it.

Today is my hardest day yet. Or maybe it is the most important. I see clearly today that I cannot do this without the love and support of the people I hold dear. When I finally reach the end, I am undone. I want to fall on the floor. I want a cold beer. Mostly, I am just in disbelief that I am still standing.

I am smiling when I check in. I walked nearly a marathon today. Through the mountains and the mud and the rain. And I did it alone. But not really.

$\mathcal{I}$ AWAKE AT FOUR IN THE MORNING. I HAVE A TRAIN to catch in an hour. I will be meeting Jamie in Porto-marín. I have a long train ride ahead of me.

I swing my feet over the side of the bed. I rub sleep from my eyes. I am covered in sweat because the presence of air-conditioning, evidently, goes against the Spanish religion. The air is stuffy, so I open the window. There is a cattle pasture behind the inn that smells like—well—a cattle pasture.

I close the window.

I check my phone. No texts. No service.

Damn this infernal thing. I am unable to call a cab to take me to the train station. This is not good. My train will be boarding soon. I am forced to use a big paper map.

Now I'm on the street, looking for a cab to flag down. But no cabs come, because it is four in the morning and nobody is awake. These are Spanish people who take naps in the middle of every day. They wake up a noon.

So I am going to have to walk to the train station. It's six miles to the depot. If I leave now on foot, I still won't make it in time. I'll have to take a much later train. This is about to turn into an all-day ordeal. There are no other options. I am going to be in transit all day.

So I start walking.

Walking hurts like fire. My calves and shins are rubber-band tight. I am in a lot of pain. I am using my cane, gimping onward, clicking on the cobblestones. The streets of Sarria are empty. The sky is black. I am walking through the city with a backpack on my shoulders, a fiddle on my back, hobbling on a walking stick.

After a few minutes of walking, my shins begin to loosen. I am still in pain, but less so. I am still using a cane, but not as aggressively. About a mile in, I am feeling pretty good. My calves are operational. Don't get me wrong, I'm in no shape to complete any marathons, but I can walk. The doctor a few villages back told me I wouldn't be able to walk for several weeks. If only he could see me now.

I arrive at an intersection downtown. The alleyways are dark. The tall, ancient buildings stretch into the dark sky, back-lit by only the stars. The tiny cars parked along the curbs form a chain stretching clear back to the horizon. The glow of various streetlamps lends a sickly orange halo to the night.

I stand at this junction with the paper map unfolded before me, leaning on my cane. My map is telling me there is a train station to my right. Five miles away. Meanwhile, at my feet, there is a bronze seashell, embedded in the pavement. A scallop shell. With an arrow pointing left. I have this feeling that envelopes me. Like a warm blanket being draped across my shoulders.

I fold the map.

I go left.

MY FEET HAVE LED ME TO THE CAMINO. MY SHOES ARE steering me, almost as if without my consent. I am on the Camino again. Walking through the ink darkness. What the hell am I doing?

I stop walking and remove my backpack. I start getting rid of things to lighten my load. I discard my spare change of clothes. I throw away my soap and toiletries. I throw away cups and bowls, books, and the bulk of my first-aid kit. I keep only my jacket, my water, a few bandages, and my fiddle. I place discarded items on the side of the trail, clothes folded, everything positioned nice and neat, with a note that reads: GOD BLESS YOU.

My pack is significantly lighter now. I am passing stone houses, pastoral farms, and herds of cattle who are still asleep. It is a clear morning, and the stars are beaming down. Being on the Camino feels like reuniting with an old friend. A friend who knows me. And I know her. She is kind. She is thoughtful. I feel safe on her highway.

I am leaning on my cane, taking strides so small they look like baby steps. But I am doing it. My heart is doing somersaults inside me. I am remembering a quote by Helen Keller, my patron saint.

"We can do anything we want to, if we stick to it long enough."

I'm praying as I walk. I remove the rosary from my pocket, the one the nun gave me. I still don't know exactly how you're supposed *do* a rosary, but I know Psalm Twenty-Three, and this is enough. I am fingering each bead, taking a deep, cleansing breath, forgetting the pain in my shins, and uttering the familiar psalm until the words have lost all meaning, until my mind becomes lost in a kind of suspended state of meditation. My mind falls into a blank state.

And I am one with the Camino.

DEAR GOD, IT'S ME AGAIN.

How have you been? How are the kids?

I know it's been a while since we talked. But praying has always been super hard for me. Nobody knows this better than you. When I was a little boy, praying was an endurance endeavor more challenging than, for example, going to JC Penney with my mother. My ADD-riddled adolescent mind liked to wander into various places during prayer, traveling into unrelated fantasy scenarios, some of which involved cowboys, pirates, or female swimwear. Within seconds I'd lose track of what I was thinking about. Kind of like what I'm doing right now.

The Lord is my shepherd, I shall not want . . .

It seems like six hundred years ago that we set out for Santiago on foot, God. And, truthfully, I don't even remember why we're out here anymore. I am tired, I am weary, and yet I am walking again. I am walking, even though it is foolishness. I am walking, even though it feels as though angry, soccer-playing toddlers have been kicking my shins for forty days and forty nights.

He maketh me to lie down in green pastures . . .

I have 150-some kilometers to Santiago from where I stand right now, God. That's what the signpost just said. One hundred and fifty freaking kilometers.

He leadeth me beside the still waters . . .

I am the only one on the trail at this hour. And I am walking so slow it's almost comical. I know, deep in my soul, that I have no business being out here on battered legs. The doctor from a few days ago, who spoke only Spanish, used a lot of big medical words I did not understand. But from what I gathered, my tibias anterior muscles, which control the entire dorsiflexion of my feet, are—if you want to get technical about this—totally screwed, Lord.

He restoreth my soul . . .

But when I saw that shell in the pavement, pointing toward the Camino, I had that warm-blanket feeling again. Whenever I get that feeling, which I don't receive *nearly* enough, I know it means something. Something carried me toward the trail. Something compelled me to walk the Camino.

Even so, the last few miles, my steps have been painful. And whenever I stop walking, I cry a little. I don't cry because of the pain, Lord. The pain is not nearly as bad as I make it out to be. Neither do I cry because I carry some great emotional burden. I think I've left a lot of mental baggage behind.

No, I cry because I'm tired. I cry because I don't know what the hell I'm doing. I cry because my phone doesn't work and I just want to talk to my wife. I cry because I feel like a consummate idiot.

I cry because I miss speaking English. I miss having conversations that don't require laser-beam focus. I miss having a discussion wherein I don't even have to *think* about what's being said, or what I'm saying, or whether I am inadvertently muttering a Spanish cussword. Fact: Spain has 1,328,900 swear words. Whereas in the US we have six cusswords, not counting *ass*.

I'm sorry I said "ass," God.

And now I've gone and said it twice.

Yea, though I walk through the Valley of the Shadow of Death…

I need your mercy. I need mercy on my legs. Mercy on my body. I need mercy on my heart and soul. I need . . . Actually, I don't know what I need. But I *do* need something. Everyone out here needs something, I guess. In fact, we pilgrims are all here because we need something. Something unnamed; something we're obviously willing to walk five hundred miles to find; something that has motivated us to undertake a challenge that only a small percentage of us will complete. We don't even know what this something is. We only seem to know that it has something to do with you.

I will fear no evil . . .

This is why we pilgrims stop at all the churches. We kneel at all the altars. We light the candles. We cross ourselves, just like our forebears did during the days when it was a federal offense to say your name. This is why we pray. We pray even though we don't know how. I don't know how.

Thy rod and thy staff, they comfort me . . .

I am leaning on my staff, walking onward to Santiago. Trying so hard to sustain my focus for more than a few minutes on one prayer, God. Even though my attention span is so painfully short. I ask humbly for things I cannot identify. And I hope sincerely that you will give me rest for my soul. But overall, I just want to hear your voice.

I don't know why I want to hear your voice. But I heard it once. I was eleven years old, half naked in a closet. And you spoke to me. Audibly. I heard it. I will always hear it. And nothing any religious fanatic can say, nothing any evangelical blowhard can claim, will ever take your words away from me.

Thou preparest a table for me, in the presence of my enemies, thou annointest my head with oil . . .

Give us weary pilgrims supernatural stamina to finish what we have set out to do, Lord. Despite our injuries. Despite our sorrows. Despite our own embarrassments. Despite our failures. Despite our conceit. Despite our selfish and greedy eyes. Help us. Help me. Somehow. Some way.

Until I hear your voice again, if I ever do, may you hear mine.

I am not a deep thinker. And the deeper thoughts I do occasionally have, I tend to keep to myself. I find them hard to articulate at times. So I don't share them. Except in this journal, I guess. But I have been on this trail for well over a month. Walking every day from can to can't. And I do have some thoughts. These thoughts might not express themselves as articulately as Sean's thoughts, but occasionally I do think.

And what I think is that I tend to be a bit of a control freak. Chalk it up to my childhood, my personality, my DNA, or whatever. It's not the best trait to have. I wish I wasn't like this. But out here, I have control over very little. Actually, I have control over nothing.

This would have turned my world upside down before. But out here. Lack of control has been freeing. Like letting go of the monkey bars only to discover the ground isn't that far beneath you. I don't want to be such a control freak.

I want to roll with the punches. I want to be flexible. I know it won't come easy. I don't know how I'll accomplish this. But it's definitely something I want to work on when I get back to the real world.

Out here on the trail you control nothing. Basically, you have three things to worry about: walking, food and water, and sleeping. The most basic human needs. A human's only needs, in fact. I have found such joy in the simplicity of only these three human needs.

I have found peace in needing nothing more. All the trappings of life have been stripped away and don't matter here. And I'm wondering whether real life is the one back home, or the one out here.

You learn things about yourself out here. Climbing mountains
that appeared ridiculously huge
from a distance; knowing your
legs carried you to the top;
rounding a bend in the road and
seeing friends you haven't seen in
a couple of days; sitting in a
field with your husband and
eating three-day-old bread that
is so hard you have to dip it in
olive juice to be able to even
bite into it; sharing a chocolate
bar with friends you just met

five minutes ago; enjoying a cold beer at the end of a long day; stopping for an impromptu picnic and everyone digging in their backpacks to share what they have; using Google translate to chat with friends along the way, and then finding that you seri- ously love each other despite the fact that you cannot under- stand each other.

It's so uncomplicated. So unbelievably beautiful. And I don't want to lose this. I don't want to lose the simplicity.

Also, you really "see" things when you are walking out here. If I had been on a bus or in a car, I would have missed them. I would have missed the old woman hanging clothes on her line with her chickens pecking at her feet. I wouldn't have seen the middle-aged woman selling homemade cheese from her kitchen window while livestock wandered down the street before her. I would have missed the farmer corralling his two cows, one of whom had no intention of going back to the stables. I never would have seen the two old ladies walking arm in arm after the Good Friday church service. Or the old man, well-dressed, fly-fishing in a stream, with the wicker fishing basket beside him.

Life is so short. I have found myself in tears thinking about this. I love our life. I love our work. I love us. But we work too much and we don't play enough. Today I am telling my-self that, when I get home, my

days will look different. I want
to seize every single moment, not
waste them. I don't know how
many moments I have left on
this earth, and I want to live
them, to really live them. I love
Sean. I want us to live these moments together.

I was thinking of all these
things when I noticed a clinking
sound coming from by backpack. I
realized that what I was hearing
was our two scallop shells gently
tapping together as I walked.
The sound followed the cadence

of my steps.

What a beautiful confirmation. A reminder that even when we aren't together, Sean and I, we are. And always will be. Not even distance can separate us. Not even time. And in my heart, I know that not even death can separate us. Life really is so simple. We are the ones who complicate it.

TODAY I WALKED TWELVE HOURS AND FORTY-TWO minutes on the Camino to Portomarín, Spain. I entered town after dark, on foot, limping, dehydrated, breathless, leaning on a walking stick. My pain had somehow subsided.

Today I prayed for twelve hours and forty-two minutes. I have never prayed for twelve hours before. I prayed as I inched forward across miles of rock and dust. I prayed with a part of my being I have never felt before. I prayed prayers that required no words.

Sometimes I was interrupted by random people who would appear behind me. They would touch my back and give me words of encouragement. They could see the grimace on my face. They saw how slowly I moved, leaning on my cane.

A Frenchman appeared in a lonesome forest and touched my shoulder. He wore no backpack. He carried no water bottle. No phone. He wore only sandals and shorts and a T-shirt. When he passed me, I saw the Chi-Ro symbol on the back of his T-shirt.

Some ladies from Brazil, who spoke only Portuguese, placed hands on my head and prayed for me, out loud, using tears to get the message across. I've never felt such kindness.

A man from Colombia saw me fingering my rosary when

he passed me. He said he wished silently in his heart that he had a rosary too. A few moments after thinking this, he found a rosary lying in the mud. He was dumbfounded. He cleaned the beads and excitedly rushed back to show them to me. He told me the story. Then we walked together for several miles, praying together, saying the Lord's Prayer in Spanish. Then he stopped praying and asked me a question.

"Are you an angel?" he said.

I snorted with laughter.

"No," I replied. "Are *you*?"

Then we both laughed together. But not that hard.

When I entered Portomarín, all our Camino friends were busy eating and drinking at sidewalk restaurants. Done for the day. They saw me entering town and the entire main street— and I mean the entire street—began to applaud. They said my name. A few of them stood. I shook hands. I hugged necks. I would have kissed babies if they'd had any.

Just then, my wife came rushing out of a nearby pizza restaurant. She had found me in the heart of Portomarín. Her smile was worth far more than twelve hours and forty-two minutes. Her smile was worth all the hours, minutes, and seconds in all eternity. She threw her arms around me. I went limp in her embrace and almost fell over.

Her first words were, "I've got you."

My cup runneth over.

PORTOMARÍN, SPAIN
TUESDAY, MAY 13, 2025

I am literally running through the street. Someone told me that Sean is in town. At first I didn't believe it. I was in a pizza restaurant at the time. I leapt up and sprinted through the town square, rounding the corner.

I see him. There on the steps of the cathedral is Sean.

I cannot even believe my eyes.

There is hot-pink kinesiology

tape wrapped around his calves.

He looks haggard, hungry, and

exhausted. But he is here, in Portomarín.

He tells me that as he was heading to the bus station this morning, the shells and yellow arrows pointing to the trail spoke to him. It took him over twelve hours to walk 22 kilometers. But he did it.

And we will be walking together again tomorrow.

I am overjoyed. Seeing him here, being near him. We will finish the Camino together. The way we started it. I don't even have words. This is the best gift I could have ever asked for. This is the happiest I can remember being in a long time. Maybe ever. We are one again.

My cup runneth over too.

EVERYONE CALLS IT SOMETHING DIFFERENT. THE Camino has many different names. The Germans call it *Jakobsweg*. The French call it the *La Chemin de St. Jacques de Compostelle*. The Chinese we've met say *Cháoshèng zhě zhī lù*, which means "Pilgrims Path." The South Koreans call it *Santiago Gill*. The Ukrainians call it *Camino Podolico*. We Americans, who speak fluent Roy Rogers, cannot help but refer to it simply as "The Trail." Which is why many of us *Americanos* say "Happy Trails" to each other, despite the ribbing we receive from sophisticated Europeans who neither understand what these words mean, nor do they know who Trigger was.

No matter the name. My wife and I have walked this path for a long time. We have been living in sweaty albergues, municipal hostels, fecal-scented dormitories, and the occasional bedbug-fumigated bunkhouse. We have been together. We have been separated. We have been high. We have been low. And, above all, we have been on our feet for most of this time.

The Camino de Santiago has been our only home. The outdoors has been our living room. Corner markets have been our kitchens. The cohort of international pilgrims, our only community.

We are a family out here. We eat together, sleep together, cry together, cook together. We watch out for each other. We walk together. We shower in the same foul stalls—sometimes at the same time. We share everything. Food. Clothing. Water. Toiletries, phone chargers, nail clippers, anti-inflammatories, books, wine, and music. We bandage each other's blisters. We loan each other euros for cups of *café*. We share pocketknives, boot laces, and even—this actually happened—sports bras.

We even share sickness. Currently, a lot of the pilgrims are sick with what is being termed "Camino Flu." The virus has been making the rounds, hopping from albergue to albergue. It's an intense, quick-moving head cold. But everyone gets a turn experiencing it. Right now, my wife has it.

And, well, that's the Camino.

When you first begin the trail, you think the most meaningful pieces of trail magic are going to come from the countryside, the villages, the spirituality, the food, the historic significance of the route, and the charming locals. But it's not about those things. The majority of your experience out here is other pilgrims. In some ways, this walk is almost entirely about them. It's more about *them* than it is about *you*. Nobody tells you this beforehand.

Some of the most powerful lessons we pilgrims have learned on this proverbial trail have not been about life or the nature of the universe. Our lessons have been in relation to each other.

How do we handle each other? How do we treat one another? How do you react to a pilgrim who has negative energy? What do you do with a toxic person? Is it wrong to leave such a pilgrim behind? Don't you still *need* them? Don't they *need* you? How do you love someone even when you can't be around them?

And where does God fit into all this Camino business? you keep wondering. How come you feel his presence so much more out here than at home? What is the reason? Is it because you're not surrounded by the trappings of ordinary modernized life? Is it because, currently, your whole world is crammed in a 32-liter backpack? Is it because, due to an overabundance of seasonal hikers, you literally have no place to lay your head tonight and therefore you must recognize the interconnected-ness of all life to survive?

You've seen these interconnected miracles firsthand. You've been stuck on the streets, about to sleep on the door-step of a closed church, when some random stranger appeared in a minivan. He spoke no English, but was fluent in human kindness. He drove you twenty minutes, found a bed for you and your wife, and asked for nothing in return.

You've been trapped in the isolated village of Rabanal, with an injury and no available beds. And the townspeople made space for you; innkeepers shuffled you from bed to bed to help you out. A local woman went to town for you and bought you new shoes, out of pure generosity. Those strangers cared about you.

And, of course, there was the miracle of you walking the trail again. You thought you were finished with the trail for-ever. You thought it was game over. But now you're walking again. You hurt, of course. But not as bad as you should be hurting.

What is this? What is this kind of miracle called? This kind of miracle would never happen in real life. So why is it hap-pening out here? Or *do* these miracles happen in real life?

Maybe this *is* real life. Maybe the life back home is the fake life. Or maybe supernatural stuff happens all the time back home. Maybe it's always around us and yet we never notice it.

I don't know.

What I do know is that we enter Santiago de Compostela at 2:11 p.m. On foot. We'd been hiking since sunup. Our pace was slow. Our clothes, threadbare. Two tired pilgrims. Forty-one days in Spain. Five hundred miles. Thousands of public toilets, none of which have been properly cleaned since the Punic Wars. We look bad. Smell bad.

Feel good.

Splintered rubber, flaking from our soles. Mud frosting our backpacks. Athletic tape is wrapped tightly around my shin-splinted legs. I clutch a cane made of wood, stabbing it onto the cobblestones with each step. For a brief moment, hobbling into Santiago, I'm not sure which century we are in. Are we modernized American tourists, trudging across twenty-first-century Spain, with smartphones in our pockets? Or are we nineth-century pilgrims, desperate and tattered, clad in sandals, clambering to see the remains of history's first martyred apostle, James?

I really can't tell you.

The cobblestone streets beneath us are ancient, polished smoothly from centuries of Reeboks, horse hooves, and bare feet. The crowded sidewalk cafés are serving lunch. Café customers begin applauding the peppered throngs of pilgrims as we march slowly past, moving toward the church spires in the distance.

"*Vaya!*" people are shouting with glee. ("Come on!")

"*Dale!*" ("Go ahead!")

"*Dale con ganas! Ya estás casi ahí!*" ("Pew! You stink!")

And then, you see it.

You see the ornate *campaña* towers, high in the distance. Taller than everything else. Reaching into the clouds. Like the hands of saints, stretching upward to touch God.

"I see it," Jamie says. "I see the cathedral tower."

"I see it too."

We both start crying.

"There it is!" we hear other pilgrims say.

Everyone is pointing into the sky.

"Look!"

"It's Santiago!"

Everyone's pace increases.

You round the corner into Obradoiro Square, which is crowded with pilgrims. Thousands. Everywhere. More pilgrims than you've ever seen in one place. Some pilgrims are cheering and jumping up and down. Some are holding each other and not saying anything. Others are lying on the pavement, smoking cigarettes or taking naps with heads resting on their packs. Everyone is marveling at the cathedral. The atmosphere is one of wonder.

Most of the pilgrims here are recent ones, those who started the trail a few days ago in Sarria. This is because the Sarria trailhead offers the shortest distance required by the

Catholic Church for earning a completion certificate. A lot of hikers who don't want to—or can't—walk the entire Camino start there. These Sarria walkers are regarded by some trail veterans as cheaters, since many of these walkers are out here purely for socialization and recreational purposes. But every pilgrim has their own reason for walking, no matter where they start from. I don't judge. I'm not smart enough to be anyone's judge.

Even so, you can tell this because their packs look brand-new. Their clothes aren't dirty. They are still fresh. But there are also long-term pilgrims among this crowd. You can spot us by the bags beneath our eyes, the mud globs clinging to our packs, the weathered looks on our faces, and the gentle glow of veneration that surrounds us. It's not jubilation. It's not amazement. We aren't taking selfies. We aren't FaceTiming. We are overcome. We're here. We're together. And that's enough.

We stand still before the medieval structure in a kind of shellshocked reverence. The cathedral stands high in an impossibly blue sky.

I fall to my knees. Not out of exhaustion. Not out of adoration. But because I *want* to be on my knees. I want to show how I feel. I feel grateful.

And then we see our friends.

"Jamie! Sean!" they're all shouting, jogging toward us. Arms open.

We are swarmed by the whole gang. All the familiar faces from the trail. The cohort of fellow pilgrims we loved along the way. We are all embracing. There are lots of laughs and tears.

There is Martin from Switzerland; we shared many walks together. We press our foreheads together and cry. There is Francisco and Monique, who attack my wife and me with a four-person hug. Julia from Germany, who weeps into my shoulder. Coline from Belgium, whose blisters are the size of quarters. Stefanie from Holland, whom we met the very first day of our walk, back in France. Suzanne, a middle-aged environmentalist from Toronto, who used homeopathic remedies to treat my swollen calves one morning in a café; who prayed aloud for me while massaging my burning muscles with her gentle hands.

And then there is Jamie. The woman I have been with for more years than I've been without her. The center of my world. The joy of my being. We, too, embrace, pressing our slick foreheads together. Saying not a word. No words are needed. Sometimes you do not need words.

In this moment, standing here before the greatest cathedral I've ever seen, I suppose I expected to feel proud. Triumphant, maybe. Like a runner who just passed the finish line. Or a guy who just won a game show. I thought I'd be over-joyed, with a major sense of completion.

But I feel none of these things.

I feel, instead, like a beggar. A small and ragged old tramp, standing before the gates of the grandest palace on earth. A tired, little man. Humiliated, injured, ugly, filthy, and destitute. But just when I can't feel any less important, or any more ridiculous or foul-smelling, I see the golden gates to Santiago are slung wide open. Open to me. Open just for me. The frail pilgrim who can barely stand.

These gates are not foreboding. They are friendly, welcoming me into the most unbelievable city. A city reminiscent of another yonder city. Where there will be joy on every face. I will receive new clothes for my body, new shoes for my battered feet, and my heavy pack will finally be removed. There, the Great Shepherd will run out to greet me. He will prepare a table for me in the presence of mine enemies. He will anoint my head with oil. Surely goodness and mercy shall follow me all the days of my life:

And I will dwell in the house of the Lord forever. And ever.

And ever.

Amen.

EPILOGO

I KEEP THINKING ABOUT THE CAMINO. IT'S ALWAYS there. Out there, existing in reality, but also within the back of my mind. In two places at once.

If my brain were a school bus, all the nerdy thoughts would be sitting up front—these are the responsible, grown-up thoughts, usually wearing horn-rimmed glasses and pocket protectors, performing important tasks on calculators, computing existentially vital equations such as, "Do BLTs actually need the L?" Meanwhile, all the cool thoughts would be sitting at the back of the bus. These back-row thoughts represent notions I never take time to examine. That's where the Camino lives.

I see the Camino from a different perspective now. When you're on the trail, you're immersed. You're living it. You can't see what it truly is because there is no "it." You're part of "it." You're saying "Buen Camino" to everyone you meet, a thousand times every hour. And they're all saying it back to you. You're speaking Spanish more than English. You walk ten hours per day sometimes, and you're removed from the daily societal game everyone plays back home. The game where everyone wears a label and has to live up to that label. You're in exotic locales, where albergue proprietors are serving you beer for breakfast without the slightest hint of irony. Townspeople call you *peregrino* when you pass by, acting as though you are doing something holy. It's bewildering.

But when you're *not* on the trail; when you're here, back at home, standing back to view the whole experience, "it" takes on a different light.

You are not the same guy you were before you started the Camino. Nobody is. Before the Camino, I rarely thought much about my own personal spirituality. I mean, don't get me wrong, I've always been a spiritual guy. Kind of. That didn't just happen overnight. There were times growing up when my spirituality was all I had. God was the only dad I ever knew. But to me, spirituality was always just a *thing*. A hobby, almost. Like yoga, kayaking, or campaigning for public office. Spirituality was just a thing humans did. But after walking the Camino, I've found that I was wrong. Being human is just a thing spirits do.

This is one of the first things you learn on the trail: that we're not human. Not actually.

I mean, of course, yes, right *now* you're human. Most of you. We are currently in physical form. Certainly. We have human lives. Human bodies. Human mothers-in-law. Human lower intestinal movements. But that's not what you *are*.

What you *are* is more than flesh and blood. You are more than a walking-talking slab of defecating meat. What you *are*, truly, is a soul.

You've always known this, of course. But knowing something is much different from experiencing it. And once you experience your own "soulness," it's a little like waking up from a dream. You realize, "Wait a second, if I am not my body, if I am more than just my thoughts, if I am indeed a soul, this means that . . ."

Yes. Exactly. It means everything.

Every day the Camino sort of lives inside me. Wherever I go, whatever I do, I think about my own soul. I remember the other souls on the Camino. I remember the camaraderie of our souls along the way. I remember the deep friendships of souls, souls who could not speak each other's human languages but discovered that love is its own language.

I think of the group of Australian soccer players who fed me when they found me hiking alone, walking ceaselessly toward my wife, leaning on my cane. I think of the young Czech woman who walked alongside me when she saw me struggling, limping with my staff, who kept pace beside me, talking cheerfully to me in her own language although I could not understand her. She didn't need me to understand her words. She just wanted me to know she was there. I think about the Franciscan friars who helped me cross a stream.

Throughout it all, I came to understand that I am not alone. And I have never been alone. Not on the trail. Not in life.

Life is not what you think it is. And life is not *about* what people say it is about. Life is neither about what you believe, nor about what you don't believe. It's not about what you gain, or about what you lose. Life is not about success or failure. Life is about people.

It's always been about people. Their love is the only thing you can take with you when you die. In short, you are the gift. You are my gift. You are my Camino.

I believe each human is hardwired to find God. We come from the factory complete with a compass inside. A compass that points True North. The good news is, this compass means you can't miss God. The bad news is, this information pisses off religious people who realize their secret handshake doesn't amount to spit.

But make no mistake, you *will* find this Great Omniscience who loves you. No matter who you are. No matter what you believe. No matter how pissed off you are at everyone else for not sharing your views.

For such abiding love is so sacred, so perpetual, so everlasting, so changeless, it doesn't even have a name. It doesn't need one. This love will outlast every earthly language, every human cult, and every rite of man. This love requires no holy book, no iconography, no relics, no list of guidelines you must follow before you're accepted into the official club. You are already in the club. You're already a member.

You are always loved. You are never alone. You will never

be alone. Don't worry if what I am saying makes no sense. It's not a big deal. Your soul understands the words even if your head doesn't.

Whenever you get discouraged, just know this: You will find what you are looking for. Even if you don't know what it is. Even if you don't know where to look. Even if you're not searching. You will find it. Because you're not chasing him. He's chasing you.

Buen Camino forever.

ABOUT THE AUTHORS

SEAN DIETRICH is a columnist, novelist, musician, and stand-up storyteller who performs regularly at the Grand Ole Opry. His work appears in publications from Maine to San Francisco and chronicles the grit and grace of Southern life. **Jamie Dietrich** is his wife, CEO, retired chef, and the steady heartbeat behind "Sean of the South." After twenty-two years of marriage, they traded the comforts of home for the dust of the Camino de Santiago—a journey that taught them that *enough* isn't a destination, but a way of being. They live with their three dogs, a houseful of instruments—which seem to procreate in the night—and a shared belief in the power of a good story.